UNDERSTANDING DREAMS
IN CLINICAL PRACTICE

The Society of Analytical Psychology Monograph Series

Hazel Robinson (Series Editor)
Published and distributed by Karnac Books

Other titles in the SAP Monograph Series

*Understanding Narcissism in Clinical Practice
in the Psychoanalytic Process*
  Hazel Robinson & Victoria Graham Fuller

*Understanding Perversion in Clinical Practice:
Structure and Strategy in the Psyche*
  Fiona Ross

*Understanding the Self–Ego Relationship in Clinical Practice:
Towards Individuation*
  Margaret Clark

Understanding Boundaries and Containment in Clinical Practice
  Rebecca Brown & Karen Stobart

Understanding Spirituality and Religion in Clinical Practice
  Margaret Clark

Orders
Tel: +44 (0)20 7431 1075; Fax: +44 (0)20 7435 9076
Email: shop@karnacbooks.com

UNDERSTANDING DREAMS IN CLINICAL PRACTICE

Marcus West

KARNAC

First published in 2011 by
Karnac Books Ltd
118 Finchley Road, London NW3 5HT

British Library Cataloguing in Publication Data

A C.I.P. for this book is available from the British Library

ISBN 978 1 85575 622 9

Edited, designed and produced by The Studio Publishing Services Ltd
www.publishingservicesuk.co.uk
e-mail: studio@publishingservicesuk.co.uk

Printed in Great Britain

www.karnacbooks.com

CONTENTS

ACKNOWLEDGEMENTS

I would like to express my enormous gratitude and thanks to those people who have kindly allowed me to describe their dreams and discuss something of our work together. I would also like to thank Hazel Robinson for her support, encouragement, and many helpful suggestions. Many thanks also to Oliver Rathbone and all at Karnac Books for their help with this book and for supporting the series as a whole. Finally, my thanks and appreciation to my family for their invaluable support and for bearing with me.

ABOUT THE AUTHOR

Marcus West is a Jungian analyst and professional member of the Society of Analytical Psychology; he works in private practice in Sussex, England. He is author of *Feeling, Being, and the Sense of Self: A New Perspective on Identity, Affect, and Narcissistic Disorders*, published by Karnac in 2007. He has published papers, taught and given talks on a range of subjects, including attachment theory, narcissism, envy, identity, and dreams. He was joint winner of the Michael Fordham Prize (2004) for his paper, "Identity, narcissism and the emotional core" and gave the Society of Analytical Psychology Annual Lecture in 2008. He has been Book Reviews Editor, and is now a member of the Editorial Board, of the *Journal of Analytical Psychology*.

To Ems, who has it

and also

to A, A, A, N, & C

This series of clinical practice monographs is being produced primarily for the benefit of trainees on psychotherapy and psychodynamic counselling courses. They are produced with the hope that they may help students a little with the psychodynamic "Tower of Babel" encountered as they embark on training.

It can be a time-consuming task for students to access all the pertinent books and papers for any one clinical subject. These single-issue monographs have been kept relatively brief and, although not comprehensive, aim to bring together some of the major theorists and their ideas in a comprehensible way, including references to significant and interesting texts.

Much of the literature provided for students of psychotherapy has been generated from four- or five-times weekly analytic work, which can be confusing for students whose courses are structured on the basis of less frequent sessions. The authors of these monographs have aimed to hold this difference in mind by offering clinical examples that are not based on intensive work.

When a training is "eclectic", that is, offering several different psychodynamic perspectives, a particular difficulty can arise with the integration—or, rather, *non*-integration—of psychoanalytic and

Jungian analytic ideas. The teaching on such trainings is often presented in blocks: a term devoted to "Freud", another to "Jung", "Klein", and so on. It is frequently the students who are left with the job of trying to see where the ideas do and do not fit together, and this can be a daunting, even depressing, experience.

SAP analysts are in a better position than most to offer some help here, because its members have been working on this kind of integration since the organization was founded in 1946. Although retaining a strong relationship with "classical" Jungian scholarship, SAP members have evolved equally strong links with psychoanalysis. Those readers who are unfamiliar with Jungian terms might wish to consult the *Critical Dictionary of Jungian Analysis* (Samuels, Shorter, & Plaut, 1986), while those unfamiliar with psychoanalytic terms may turn to *The Language of Psychoanalysis* (Laplanche & Pontalis, 1973).

The authors are Jungian analysts who have trained at the Society of Analytical Psychology, with extensive experience of teaching both theory and practice. We are indebted to our patients. Where a patient's material is recognizable, their permission to publish has been given. In other cases, we have amalgamated and disguised clinical material to preserve anonymity. We have also borrowed gratefully from the work of our supervisees in many settings.

We thank Karnac Books for their continued support and patience in bringing the series to publication. I want to end by thanking my colleagues within the SAP for their work so far—and for their work to come.

Hazel Robinson
Series Editor

CHAPTER ONE

An overview of dreaming

"Dreams are the royal road to the unconscious"

(Freud, 1900a, p. 607)

D reams have been considered an important source of wisdom and knowledge by all the great civilizations and religious traditions of which we have a written record, whether their meaning has been taken to be a message from God, a prophetic foretelling of future events, or a revelation of hidden knowledge. At other times, notably in some quarters of the scientific community in the past century, the wisdom of dreams has been doubted and dismissed as incomprehensible nonsense or "froth", a debate which continues to this day to some extent, although most of the arch-sceptics now acknowledge that dreams have personal meaning and reflect the individual's personality and waking concerns.

In this book, I explore these claims and counter-claims and focus specifically on how the counsellor, therapist, or analyst might consider, address, and work with the dreams that our clients bring. I introduce a simple, effective, and, I would also suggest, profound method of understanding and working with dreams, based upon the network of associations related to the symbolic nature of dream images and dream narratives. I draw particularly on the work of the two great depth psychologists of the twentieth century, Sigmund Freud and Carl Jung, as well as many other psychoanalysts, psycho-therapists, neuroscientists, and dream researchers who have contributed to our understanding of dreams and dreaming.

In the modern era, Freud was the first to really take up the subject of dreams in his monumental book, published in 1900, *The Interpretation of Dreams*, which not only set out a comprehensive theory for understanding and interpreting dreams, but also laid down some of the foundation stones of psychoanalytic theory. Freud saw dreams as "the royal road to the unconscious", which, I think, is one of the great quotes relating to dreams.[1]

In his attempt to understand the sometimes bizarre imagery and style of dreams, Freud proposed that the dream has a surface "manifest" content that disguises a hidden "latent" content; he saw this latent content, which is uncovered in the process of working on the dream, as the real meaning of the dream. For example, he interpreted the following recurring dream that a woman had had as a young girl (she was the youngest in the family):

> All her brothers, sisters and cousins, who had been romping in a field, suddenly grew wings, flew away and disappeared.

Freud saw the manifest content of the dream (the children growing wings and flying away) as disguising the latent content (the hostile wishes of the young girl toward her siblings). His interpretation of the dream was, therefore, that the girl wished that her siblings would "become angels", in other words, die and no longer be in competition with her (Freud, 1900a, p. 252). He suggested that this dream represented the fulfilment of a wish (to kill off her brothers, sisters, and cousins) that the child had been unable to accept consciously, so that she had had to repress this terrible thought.

If Freud first took on the subject of dreams, it was Jung who made it his own, with his enthusiasm for dreams and his belief that they were uniquely able to tell us about what is most important within ourselves. His view echoed that of the ancients, that dreams hold a pre-eminent wisdom that can offer us invaluable guidance if only we are able to understand them and heed them.

Jung disagreed with Freud's view of dreams. He did not think that dreams attempted to disguise hidden wishes; he thought, rather, that they show us "the unvarnished, natural truth", and that one of their prime functions is to correct the limited, narrow view of ourselves that regularly we come to hold. This is his view of "compensation", which I outline in more detail later on.

Jung understood the sometimes bizarre and incomprehensible nature of dream images to be due to the fact that they are symbols. Jung said that when we can understand and interpret the image symbolically, we can then understand its meaning, although he would have added that, as a symbol, an image's meaning can carry on unfolding;[2] in other words, that we can find many rich layers of meaning in a symbolic image—one can still be working on the same dream or dream image for years, indeed, for one's whole life! Chapter Ten deals with initial dreams, and explores a dream that went on unfolding throughout the course of a therapy.

So, in regard to the child's dream of her siblings growing wings, flying off, and disappearing, Jung would have agreed with Freud that this was a symbolic image that could relate to them becoming angels. He might have interpreted, however, that as well as a potential death wish, the dream also expresses a possible envy of her siblings' power and abilities (symbolized by their ability to fly in the dream), as well as a feeling of abandonment and loneliness as they fly off and disappear. She might have experienced this abandonment and loneliness when they went off to play their older-children games, leaving her, the youngest, feeling stranded and alone, or perhaps the dream was also "working through" the consequences of her death wish: perhaps she already felt abandoned and lonely through having killed them off in her mind.

Jung was very much attracted to Freud's new psychoanalytic theories and it was, in fact, Freud's book, *The Interpretation of Dreams*, that led Jung to contact him, so that Jung became Freud's ardent follower and staunchest ally for a number of years, while the two worked, with others, to establish psychoanalysis as a new science. As I have said, Jung did not think that dreams were always and essentially wish-fulfilments, although he would allow that they could be on occasion if that represented a compensation for the dreamer's conscious attitude (take, for example, the dual interpretation of the "flying off" dream above). Jung's later view, that dreams are "a spontaneous self-portrayal, in symbolic form, of the actual situation in the unconscious" (Jung, 1948[1916], par. 505), emphasizes the ability of dreams to show us ourselves and our situation as it really is.

Jung's main disagreement with Freud was that he thought Freud interpreted dreams in a formulaic manner, interpreting their rich symbolic content in terms of a limited number of meanings related usually to Freud's predominant interest in sexuality. Jung thus accused Freud of being reductionist, treating a richly symbolic image as simply a sign with a sexual or aggressive meaning. This difference of view in regard to the role of sexuality was one of the main reasons that the two split from each other, irrevocably, in 1913. Jung had other criticisms, which I outline below.

I explore both Jung's and Freud's views in this book, and I hope to show how both can contribute to a fuller understanding of dreams. In Chapter Eleven, I also, as an illustration, give a detailed reading of a dream of one of Freud's patients, who became known as the Wolf Man, in both a Freudian and a Jungian idiom.

Following the work of these pioneers of dream exploration, there was a backlash against what became, for a while, the dominant understanding that dreams had meaning, and particularly against Freud's view that dreams were disguised wish-fulfilments (Freud also held that the purpose of dreams was to allow the dreamer to sleep undisturbed by the motivational "id" urges such as sex or hunger). I detail the fascinating arguments and counter-arguments in Chapter Twelve, and particularly draw out what the dream researchers and neuroscientists have contributed to our understanding of dreams; here, however, I confine myself to a brief outline of the arguments in so far as they help us locate the positions at this time.

In 1953, two dream researchers, Aserinsky and Kleitman, found that the brain was particularly activated during what they described as REM (rapid eye movement) sleep, and they suggested that dreaming was associated with this period of sleep. It has turned out subsequently that although most dreams occur during this period, dreaming also occurs in what is called non-REM sleep. However, these and other discoveries began a shift away from an analysis of, and interest in, the *content* of dreams, and more toward an analysis of the *form and function* of dreams.

One popular theory put forward by Hobson and McCarley in 1977, which was much taken up by the press at the time, suggested that dreams were triggered by a very primitive part of the brain known as the pons, which is common to all mammals (it is believed that certain animals also dream, as well as having periods of REM sleep). Hobson and McCarley proposed an "activation-synthesis" theory of dreams, which held that dreams were simply *activated* by the random firing of this primitive part of the brain, which triggers images that the higher brain tries to *synthesize* into some kind of story, hence many dreams seem like strange fragments cobbled together. The dream is, they suggest, simply the higher brain trying to make sense of what is, essentially, nonsense. For these theorists this accounted for the frequently bizarre nature of dreams, dream images, and dream narratives.

Once again, however, the early hypothesis turned out to be incorrect, and it has subsequently been shown that the more developed, "higher" functioning of the brain is essential to dreaming and, in fact, it is when these parts of the brain are damaged due to trauma or brain disease that dreaming ceases altogether (Solms & Turnbull, 2002).

Regarding the *content* of dreams, of which probably hundreds of thousands have been collected over the years in and out of dream laboratories, there were a significant number of dream researchers who did not follow Hobson and McCarley's activation–synthesis theory, yet who also became critical of the dominant Freudian view of dreams. These researchers felt there was no evidence for the suggestion that there is an attempt to disguise the meaning of dreams and that, furthermore, the evidence from neuroscientists suggested there was no mechanism in the brain that is involved in dreaming which could perform the censorship that would have been required for such disguise (see Domhoff, 2004, for a discussion of both these points).

These dream researchers argue that the content of dreams is usually understandable, although they often represent "novel constructions" (Domhoff, 2004, p. 12); Domhoff concludes that dreams "reflect or express more than they disguise" and suggests that the bizarreness in dreams may be due to the same kind of figurative thinking that produces metaphor, conceptual blending, and irony in waking life (Lakoff, 1977, p. 90, quoted in Domhoff, 2004). Hobson (2005), an arch anti-Freudian, similarly explains the potentially bizarre nature of dreams as due to the sleeping mind making "too many associations", and he describes dreaming as a "hyperassociative state".

Freud's views also came in for criticism and revision from within the psychoanalytic tradition, with Donald Meltzer suggesting that, in trying to prove that dreams were not nonsense, Freud was led into "a type of logical error, namely of confusing obscurity of meaning with cryptic or hidden meaning" (Meltzer, 1983, p. 12).

Later, I suggest that Jung's understanding of dreams holds up particularly well in regard to these discoveries of dream researchers, and that in suggesting that dreams are not disguised, and in pointing to the hyperassociative, figurative thinking that goes on in dreaming, these theorists are, in fact, describing the abstracting, symbol-making function of the mind. I argue that this is precisely the essence of Jung's theory of dreaming: the difficulty in understanding a dream is in the difficulty in understanding the symbolic nature of the image that the dream has created. It is this process that I concentrate on in this book.

Notes

1. In fact, the full quote is, "The interpretation of dreams is the royal road to a knowledge of the unconscious activities of the mind" (Freud, 1900a, p. 607); the commonly quoted abbreviated version does have a better ring to it.

2. Or, as Jung puts it more poetically, "A symbol does not define or explain; it points beyond itself to a meaning that is darkly divined yet still beyond our grasp, and cannot be adequately expressed in the familiar words of our language" (Jung, 1926, par. 644).

CHAPTER TWO

A brief outline of Freud's views on dreams

"Dreams are often most profound when they seem most crazy"

(Freud, 1900a, p. 443)

In 1900, at the beginning of the new century, Freud auspiciously published *The Interpretation of Dreams*. Over time, he came to believe that this book was the most important of all his writings. It not only presented a method of understanding and analysing dreams, but laid down some of the foundation stones of psychoanalytic theory.

The book is long and complex. In it he first gives an overview of both the classical and popular methods of dream interpretation as well as the scientific views of the day (Freud, 1900a, Chapter 1). The ancient view was that dreams were a message from an external source, a superior power, which could be deciphered with reference to an understanding of symbols and, furthermore, that dreams foretell the future (see also Blechner, 2001, pp. 6 ff.); Macrobius and Artemidorus of Daldis modified this view, believing that there were two classes of dreams, one influenced by the past and present, one related to the future (Freud, 1900a, p. 2). These views were challenged by Aristotle, who held that dreams did not come from a divine agency, and were not prophetic (see Chapter Five).

The scientific view of Freud's time was divided between those who thought dreams continued the preoccupations of waking life and those who believed they were an escape from it; some thought they had no psychological significance but were randomly generated by mental stimuli (a precursor of Hobson and McCarley's views) (Freud, 1900a, pp. 21 ff.).

The second section of the book describes the nature of dreaming and Freud's method of interpreting dreams. He proposed that dreams originated from the unconscious of the dreamer and had personal meaning that could be understood through the method of free association (whereby the person says whatever comes to mind in relation to a particular dream, word, image, or feeling). He had developed this method, and his concept of the unconscious, in his first writings and work on hysteria, published a few years earlier (Freud & Breuer, 1895d). This view that dreams had personal meaning generated from the psyche of the dreamer has been the dominant theory since that time, despite having its detractors.

Freud proposed that dreams are disguised; that there is a manifest content—the dream as told by the dreamer with its frequently bizarre narrative and imagery—and a latent, hidden content, which only becomes clear following analysis of the dream. He proposed that this disguise is brought about through the process of "dream-work", which acted so as to censor the unacceptable wishes expressed by the dream. He proposed that dreams are, in fact, the expression of frustrated (suppressed or repressed) wishes.

Freud thought that the reason these wishes had to be disguised was that they relate to unacceptable, often sexual impulses (he thought that although the "majority" of the dreams of adults dealt with "sexual material and gave expression to erotic wishes", he explicitly stated that by no means all do (ibid., pp. 395–396)). In discussing these wishes and the murderous nature of some dreams relating, for example, to the death of loved relatives, he introduced a theory that was to become central to psychoanalysis: the Oedipus complex. To illustrate it, he gave the example of an adult patient who had had the following dream at the age of four: "A lynx or fox was walking on the roof; then something had fallen down or (the dreamer) had fallen down; and then her mother was carried out of the house dead" (Freud 1900a, p. 258).

His patient remembered the dream tearfully and said that her relations must think her horrible. Freud interpreted that when she was a child she had wished that she could see her mother dead. The patient had responded immediately by saying that she had once been called "lynx-eye" by a "street urchin" and that, when she was three, a tile, falling from the house, had struck her mother, making her head bleed violently. Freud then goes on to discuss the Oedipus complex, where the child unconsciously wishes one parent dead so that they can have the other parent exclusively for themselves.

Freud proposed that dream-work operated unconsciously through a number of mechanisms, which he described as: condensation, displacement, and representability, which I will outline below.[1] He also thought that in telling the dream the dreamer begins to distort its content in order to make it more coherent and rational and to give it a narrative flow; he called this process "secondary revision". Freud stressed later that he thought it was the dream-work, not the latent content, which was the essence of the dream (Freud, 1923c), and that it was the work of unravelling the dream-work that led to the meaning of the dream, as I shall explain further below.[2]

In the above dream, we can see how the symbol of the "lynx or fox" *condenses* (brings together) the image of the dreamer (lynx-eye), something cunning or sly (the fox), and someone on the roof which causes something (the tile) to fall (these three associations have been "condensed" into one image); similarly the dream *displaces* the responsibility for the falling (and killing) action onto the lynx/fox, in other words, "it wasn't me, it was the lynx/fox that did it!" The whole idea has been *represented* and *dramatized* (a term Freud introduced soon after (1901a)) by the dream, which thus (cleverly) represents and disguises the wish to kill off the dreamer's mother.

Freud concluded that, ultimately, the purpose of dreaming was to preserve sleep as the conscious mind cannot cope with these infantile wishes and drives and so represses them. In Chapter VII of the book, Freud finally outlines and delineates the Unconscious, Preconscious, and Conscious areas of the mind, where censorship/repression controls what is allowed to become conscious (it was not until 1923 that he proposed that this censorship was carried out by what he then called the superego (Freud, 1923b)).

I end this brief introduction to Freud's views on dreaming with a brief example of one of his patient's dreams: "At her summer holiday resort, by the Lake of ——, she dived into the dark water just where the pale moon was mirrored in it" (Freud, 1900a, p. 399).

A summary of Freud's understanding of the dream is as follows (note that this interpretation comes from Freud himself, following a stream of free associations from the dream): Freud saw this as a "birth dream" as he reversed the event reported in the manifest dream, so that "diving into the water" becomes "coming out of the water", in other words, being born. A child is born, he reasoned, from the bottom, for which the French word *"lune"*, meaning "pale moon", is used in slang.

Freud, therefore, asked his patient why she might be wishing to be born at her summer holiday resort. She replied "without hesitation" that she had felt reborn through the therapy with him. He concluded that the dream was an invitation to him to continue treating her at the holiday resort, in other words, to visit her there. He added that perhaps there is a hint of the patient's wish to become a mother herself (how much she might wish Freud to be the father of the child he does not say). The dream's primary wish-fulfilment, however, is that there would not be a break in the treatment for the holiday and Freud would visit her at her holiday resort.

This interpretation demonstrates the mechanisms of condensation and displacement, as all these meanings were condensed into the imagery of the dream. The condensation here is relatively succinct; Freud points out that on some occasions, a dream that may be written out in half a page might generate associations which "may occupy six, eight, or a dozen times as much space" (*ibid.*, p. 278).

In contrast to Jung's attitude to dreams, to which I now turn, Freud's method was to follow the stream of free associations in order to undo the "dream-work" which had disguised the meaning of the dream. The meaning lay, for Freud, as much in the stream of associations leading away from the dream as in the dream itself, by which I mean that the dream is merely the jumping-off point for the stream of associations rather than containing a richly packed set of symbolic meanings, as Jung believed (see Chapter Three); as stated above, Freud thought that the dream-work was the essence of the dream.

Notes

1. He later elaborated five functions of the unconscious: condensation, displacement, timelessness, absence of mutual contradiction, and replacement of external by internal reality (1915e). In Chapter Four, I describe how Matte Blanco distilled these five characteristics into one, which is that the unconscious recognizes the symmetry—the sameness—between things, and I suggest that this offers a way of understanding the formation of symbols in a way that encompasses and can reconcile both Freud's and Jung's views on dreams and dreaming.

2. This view was probably partly a criticism of Jung's position, as he would have been one of those whom Freud characterized as having an excessive respect for the "mysterious unconscious" (Freud, 1923c, p. 111).

CHAPTER THREE

A brief outline of Jung's views on dreams

"Dreams are impartial, spontaneous products of the unconscious psyche, outside the control of the will. They are pure
nature; they show us the unvarnished, natural truth, and are
therefore fitted, as nothing else is, to give us back an attitude
that accords with our basic human nature when our consciousness has strayed too far from its foundations and run into an
impasse"

(Jung, 1934a, par. 317)

Jung's essential attitude was one of respect for the dream itself. He
felt that Freud's method of free association could lead away from
the dream (Jung, 1934b, par. 320), while he was interested in what
the dream itself had to say and what it symbolized for the dreamer;
for example, in the dream described at the end of the previous chapter the image of "diving into the dark water just where the pale moon
was mirrored in it", is hardly explored at all, and certainly not by the
dreamer, as Freud worked from his own associations to the image
(that it symbolized being born).

Jung's attitude to dreams linked back more to the tradition of the
ancients, as he believed that the dream did offer a kind of special

knowledge, but not one that came from a traditional "superior power" or "external source". For him, the dream comes "as if from outside" because it comes from the part of us that is unconscious, which is experienced as both a part of us and apart from us. For Freud, this unconscious part operated to disguise wishes (as in dreams) and disrupt the ego; for Jung, it was more constructive, and was trying to inform the ego and present new formulations of the future personality (Astor, 2002). He called this part of us "the self", which he thought of as that part of our personality that guides us, and our development, in a process that he called "individuation" (see the companion volume in this series, *Understanding the Self-Ego Relationship in Clinical Practice: Towards Individuation* by Margaret Clark (2006)).

Jung believed that our view and understanding of what is going on in ourselves and our lives, as held consciously by our ego, is inevitably narrow. He thought that we too readily become wedded to this narrow view, perhaps because there are things we simply have not envisaged or experienced, or due to a wish to keep out uncomfortable insights or parts of ourselves we would rather not acknowledge (he called these the "shadow" aspects of ourselves). The parts we do not want to acknowledge correspond with the parts Freud thought we repressed, although Jung thought that the unconscious was not simply the "dustbin" for the repressed elements of the psyche, but also contained new elements of the psyche which were pressing to become incorporated in the personality. If we can listen to and incorporate these other elements of the psyche, we reach a more complete picture of ourselves; in other words, the process of individuation allows us to include ever more elements of our personalities.

Jung thought that dreams play a vital role in this process. He thought that they show us the "natural, unvarnished truth" and that they are "therefore fitted, as nothing else is, to give us back an attitude that accords with our basic human nature when our consciousness has strayed too far from its foundations and run into an impasse" (Jung, 1934a, par. 317). The best we can do with dreams is to learn to listen to what the dream itself has to tell us.

Jung thought that dreams present symbols and commentaries pointing to these unacknowledged and denied parts of ourselves and, thus, are *compensations* for our current, narrow, conscious attitudes. As he put it:

> [Dreams] do not deceive, they do not lie, they do not distort or disguise, but naïvely announce what they are and what they mean. They are irritating and misleading only because we do not understand them. . . . We can also see what it is that makes them so strange and so difficult: for we have learned from experience that they are invariably seeking to express something that the ego does not know and does not understand. [Jung, 1946, par. 189]

While for Freud dreams were wish-fulfilments, for Jung they offered a compensatory picture to the dreamer's current conscious attitude.[1] In other words, dreams are trying to tell us something new; as von Franz put it, "dreams don't waste much spit telling us what we already know" (1980).

Some of the complexity of dreams is due to the fact that the symbolic images can be interpreted on different levels and frequently on more than one level at the same time. If we take an apparently simple dream that someone has of "meeting their uncle unexpectedly" (more of a dream fragment, really), we can see how it might be taken on four different levels, as Jung described (Jung, 1917, pars 130 ff.):

- *the objective level,* where the dream image of the uncle refers to the uncle as he is in reality, or someone symbolically similar to him;
- *the subjective level,* where the dream image of the uncle refers to a part of the dreamer that is subjectively like the uncle in some way;
- *the archetypal level,* where the dream of the uncle would refer to some universal quality that might be shared by many or all uncles, for example, being friendly and "avuncular" (or the opposite); this may be elucidated or "amplified" in relation to a myth or cultural theme, for example, the untrustworthy uncle who kills the king and marries the queen in Shakespeare's *Hamlet*, or the abusing uncle in The Who's musical *Tommy*;
- *the transference level,* where the relationship to the figures in the dream describe something of the relationship to the therapist at that time; for example, the therapist is experienced as avuncular or like the dreamer's actual uncle or like an untrustworthy, abusing uncle (very importantly, as we shall see, it is necessary to ask the dreamer themselves for their associations to their uncle and/or uncles in general).

If dreams were simply about the realistic object as it appears in the dream, here, the uncle, the image would hardly be symbolic at all. It is the ability of the dream image to represent and stand for something else that makes it symbolic. The man-in-the-street's understanding of the dream takes the dream images on the objective level very concretely, which frequently makes the dream sound bizarre or at least peculiar: "I dreamt about my uncle last night, which was weird as I haven't seen him for years, why on earth did I dream about him?"

We look at these different levels in detail in Chapter Five, but before I do that I will look, in the next chapter, at the symbolic nature of dreams and why it is that the unconscious operates in this way. In order to round off this introduction to Jung's views on dreams, however, I will look at one of Jung's own dreams, which will also have the benefit of drawing attention to the fact that Jung described certain dreams as "archetypal" not only when they touch on universal, archetypal themes, but also when they are particularly powerful and important. We can all probably remember dreams that seem more striking, more luminous, more memorable than others. Dreams such as these can, and sometimes quite literally do, change the direction of the dreamer's life.

These dreams often come at a point where the person's "old way" has become outmoded or stuck, they have come to an impasse, as Jung puts it, and the dream can bring to consciousness the new insight or direction that has been brewing in the person's unconscious. The person perhaps has a sense that something is not quite right, or perhaps even that something is very wrong and needs to change, but they cannot quite put their finger on what it is. Dreams are often unique in being able to do just this. This does raise the question of whether the individual would have come to their realization anyway, without the help of the dream, a question I will look at in Chapter Six (an allied question is whether dreams need to be remembered and interpreted to be effective, something I also discuss).

Jung had the following dream at around the time he was becoming disillusioned with Freud and was probably unconsciously, if not consciously, considering breaking from him. This was just such an archetypal, "big" dream that signalled the future direction that Jung was to take; as a "bonus" it was a dream that he told Freud and, indeed, we have Freud's reaction to the dream as well as Jung's interpretation of it. Jung describes the dream as follows:

I was in a house I did not know, which had two storeys. It was "my house". I found myself in the upper storey, where there was a kind of salon furnished with fine old pieces in rococo style. On the walls hung a number of precious old paintings. I wondered that this should be my house, and thought, "Not bad". But then it occurred to me that I did not know what the lower floor looked like. Descending the stairs, I reached the ground floor. There everything was much older, and I realised that this part of the house must date from about the fifteenth or sixteenth century. The furnishings were medieval; the floors were of red brick. Everywhere it was rather dark. I went from one room to another thinking, "Now I really must explore the whole house". I came upon a heavy door, and opened it. Beyond it I discovered a stone stairway that led down into the cellar. Descending again, I found myself in a beautifully vaulted room which looked exceedingly ancient. Examining the walls, I discovered layers of brick among the ordinary stone blocks, and chips of brick in the mortar. As soon as I saw this I knew that the walls dated from Roman times. My interest was now intense. I looked more closely at the floor. It was on stone slabs, and in one of these I discovered a ring. When I pulled it, the stone slab lifted, and again I saw a stairway of narrow stone steps leading down into the depths. These, too, I descended, and entered a low cave cut into the rock. Thick dust lay on the floor and in the dust were scattered bones and broken pottery, like remains of a primitive culture. I discovered two human skulls, obviously very old and half disintegrated. Then I awoke. [Jung, 1963, pp. 182–183]

Jung said that it was plain to him that the house represented an image of the psyche—that is to say, the state of his consciousness at the time, with hitherto unconscious additional levels. Consciousness was represented by the salon, which had an inhabited atmosphere, in spite of its antiquated style. The ground floor stood for the first level of the unconscious. The deeper he went, the more alien and dark the scene became. In the cave, he discovered the remains of a primitive culture, the world of the primitive man within himself,

> a world that can scarcely be reached or illuminated by consciousness . . . the primitive psyche of man borders on the life of the animal soul, just as the caves of prehistoric times were usually inhabited by animals before man laid claim to them. [ibid., p. 184]

This dream can be understood as a blueprint for Jung's future understanding of the psyche, which differed from Freud's view. For

Jung, the lower levels of the house/psyche—the unconscious—were not simply the levels where we put those parts of ourselves that we do not want to know, all the repressed ideas, as Freud thought. Rather, for Jung, these parts of the unconscious are culturally rich, carrying the wisdom of primitive man; for example, the Roman period in the dream could refer to Roman culture. Jung was very much interested in what "primitive man" could tell us; he particularly thought that modern man had become dissociated from our instinctual nature and that we had become prone to intellectualization. He thought that the Greek and Roman cultures (among many others) could tell us an enormous amount about ourselves, and he found their myths and legends a particularly rich source of knowledge.

For him, this represented the archetypal knowledge that we hold in common with our ancestors. They, too, had to balance the face we show to the world, which Jung called the persona, with the parts that we wish to deny or that are undeveloped, which he called the shadow. They, too, had the task of finding their way in the world and meeting the threats to their survival and maturation; Jung saw this as the ego's natural task and journey, which is described in the heroes' journeys of myths and legends. The ancients also had spiritual experience and a relationship with their god or gods, which was embodied in their religious beliefs and practices.

Rather than seeing these as "primitive" beliefs, or stories which had nothing to tell us, Jung realized that we are struggling with similar issues to those of these earlier cultures and civilizations, as well as many other contemporary non-Western cultures. He thought that their myths and legends often described the exact same struggles from which we can learn much and in which we can discern the same archetypal patterns of knowledge and behaviour.

In relation to Jung's dream, and, as a contrast, Jung reports that Freud was chiefly interested in the two skulls in the cave and says that he questioned Jung as to what he thought about them and who they were. Jung thought that Freud believed that he, Jung, had a deeply buried death wish towards Freud, something that would have been predicted by Freud's understanding of the Oedipus complex, where Jung would have been seen as the son trying to kill off the father. As a result, Jung knowingly disguised his answer, saying that he thought the two skulls might refer to his wife and his sister-in-law—Freud no doubt saw through this disguise!

Father vs mother in Freud is symbolic

So, while Jung interpreted this dream largely on the subjective and archetypal levels (as what it said about his subjective internal world and how that related to universal themes), Freud interpreted it largely on the transference level (relating to himself and Jung). And yet, seeing that this dream was dreamt at a time when Jung was becoming increasingly conscious of his differences from Freud and of his disagreement with Freud's views, perhaps the dream *did* symbolize a death wish towards Freud to some extent, and that Freud was right.

However, what is clear from the dream is that, in laying out Jung's future view of the psyche, the dream could have symbolized an archetypal representation of the psyche which was, at the same time, the means by which Jung would "kill off" Freud and his views. In other words, *both* interpretations could be true and could complement each other and lead to a fuller understanding of the dream. Jung could be thought to be "killing off" Freud with his new and different understanding of the psyche.

Throughout this book, we shall see that more than one interpretation of a dream is possible and that the different interpretations, often on the different levels I have described, can lead to a fuller understanding of the symbolic meanings embedded in the dream. Mark Blechner (2001, p. 7) reports that there is an old Talmudic story that Rabbi Bana'ah told a dream to twenty-four dream interpreters and that each gave a different interpretation, making a different prediction, and that all of them were right!

Jung vs. Freud, or Jung and Freud?

Jung and Freud both thought that dreams have personal meaning and that their origins lie in parts of our selves that are unconscious. For Freud, these were largely repressed instinctual "id" urges, which press to be satisfied and which must be held in check by the ego and its defences. For Jung, these were parts of the self which function largely constructively and which press to be included in the personality. This divergence is reflected particularly in their views of dreams, where the dream is seen either as a product of the unconscious which aims to disguise a wish-fulfilment through dream-work, or as an open and direct expression of a new element of the psyche.

In the next chapter, I will look at the work of the psychoanalyst Matte Blanco, who analysed Freud's understanding of the unconscious and proposed a view of its functioning that, I suggest, offers a reconciliation of the two views: specifically, whether the disguise that Freud describes might not, in fact, be a product of the process of forming a symbol. When one understands the dream images as symbols, and how to interpret those symbols, Jung and Freud's views no longer conflict in the same way.

Furthermore, the divergence could be oversimplified in terms of whether the elements of the unconscious are seen to function constructively (Jung) or destructively (Freud). I suggest here that, in so far as every dream introduces a new element of the psyche, it is destructive and disruptive to the old order of things, to the status quo of the ego, as well as being constructive to the extent that it is a new addition and as long as, and in so far as, it is able to be integrated with the current view of the individual as held by the ego; for this the ego must be flexible (see West, 2008 for a fuller discussion of ego-functioning).

Whether the new element of the psyche is described as an aggressive or sexual impulse or an aspect of the individual's hitherto undeveloped sensual nature (or even their spiritual nature), both need to be known about and, thereby, integrated into/with the ego. Nightmares and recurring dreams are examples of where the psyche is having particular difficulty in integrating these new elements with the ego (see Chapter Thirteen).

In this book, I follow Jung in staying close to the dream imagery itself and being guided by the dreamer's associations to the dream, in other words, making the dream and its symbolism central. I believe this model largely reflects the creative kernel of both Jung's and Freud's views and offers a practical technique for working with dreams.

It is worth noting that Freud and Jung were writing in the early part of the twentieth century and that psychoanalysis has come a long way since that time, most notably in recognizing the central importance of relationships in human development and functioning. This work has led to the development of *object relations theory*, which throws a critical light on both Freud's view that the instincts, and, in particular, the sexual instincts, are the central organizing principle of human life, and Jung's view that the central organizing principle is the development of the individual's own self.[2] These two views are not overthrown by understanding the centrality of relationship, but need to be seen as secondary and subject to it.[3] Dreams can be understood to be particularly helpful in elucidating patterns of relationship (see the following chapters) and, therefore, reflect exactly the preoccupations of object relations theory regarding the importance of relationship.

Notes

1. Although, as he also said, "In putting forward a compensation theory I do not wish to assert that this is the only possible theory of dreams or that it completely explains *all* the phenomena of dream-life" (Jung, 1948[1916], par. 491).

2. As Fairbairn (1940) argued, we do not have relationships to have sex, we have sex in order to have relationships (paraphrased); a critique of Jung's view would be that the individual's self is only properly developed in relationship, and that that development is ultimately only fulfilling in so far as it is directed toward relationship; as the Zulu maxim puts it, "a person is a person through (other) persons" (an element of the African concept of Ubuntu).

3. It is from this object relations theory perspective that Meltzer (1983) has offered a thoroughgoing criticism and major revision of Freud's understanding of dreams (see Chapter Fourteen).

CHAPTER FOUR

The language of dreams:
the symbolic and the unconscious

"The most skilful interpreter of dreams is he who has the faculty of observing resemblances"

(Aristotle, 1941, pars 464b, 7–8)

The most valuable and immediately useful thing I have learnt in my career as a psychotherapist (so far) is how and why the unconscious works the way it does. This not only has an immediate significance and application for understanding dreams and the nature of symbols, but I have also found it invaluable in understanding all manner of behaviours and difficulties with which we struggle as human beings, and which had previously been either mysterious or downright incomprehensible to me.

My understanding largely comes from the work of the South American psychoanalyst, Ignacio Matte Blanco, who explored Freud's five characteristics of the unconscious,[1] as outlined in *The Interpretation of Dreams* (1900a) and "The unconscious" (1915e), and concluded that the unconscious functioned by recognizing the sameness—what he called the "symmetry"—between one thing and another (Matte Blanco, 1975, 1988). In an earlier book (West, 2007), I explored some of the clinical ramifications of this understanding and linked it, in particular, to recent developments in attachment theory, infant development research, and neuroscience.

I will put this understanding of the functioning of the unconscious as succinctly as possible here, relating it to child development issues, and hope you will find it useful in itself, as well as in relation to understanding dreams.

The infant is sensitive to change, sameness, and difference and, at first, will seek out and prefer experiences which are as similar as possible to the previous good experiences that he or she has had (Matte Blanco, 1977; Watson, 1994, 1995): for example, experiences of nurture, warmth, positive interaction, and care. The infant needs to be able to do this in order to begin to recognize the world around him or her, to navigate through it, to seek out good experience and avoid bad experience where possible, and to categorize experiences, understand them, and interact with others. This is primarily in the service of making a good attachment to the infant's primary care-givers. The infant is all the time, therefore, categorizing and "appraising" his or her experience (Bowlby, 1969).

We can see that it will be practically very helpful, perhaps even evolutionarily vital, to be able to recognize in any particular circumstance the similarities with earlier experience: "Is this person being helpful and kindly, or threatening and dangerous, like others on previous occasions?" This scanning and appraisal of experience goes on all the time unconsciously and, in fact, in any one day, we usually have too much experience to be able to successfully digest, so that an important function of sleep and dreaming is to help us digest and process this experience. As the psychoanalyst Donald Meltzer (1983) puts it, "dreaming is unconscious thinking".

In terms of dreams and symbolization, therefore, we can see that it will be very helpful to be able to recognize that, for example, this new counsellor with whom I have just started working is similar to the kindly, helpful uncle with whom I grew up and had a long, friendly, and constructive relationship. Or, similarly, to realize that through the work of the counselling I am beginning to operate in a more kindly, helpful, and constructive way towards myself, reminiscent of my uncle's attitude towards me when I was growing up, rather than behaving in the uncooperative and self-destructive way that I have been doing until recently. (I am pre-empting here some of the conclusions of the next chapter and have just described interpretations of the uncle dream on the transference and the subjective levels.)

A dream image is "constructed", therefore, simply because there is a shift in the image—an association—that has meaning. If we deconstruct the uncle dream, it could be spelt out as follows: the dreamer has recently begun counselling and is unconsciously concerned with trustworthiness and helpfulness and, specifically, with the issue of how trustworthy and helpful their new counsellor is. The dreamer's experience has been of people not being very helpful or trustworthy in the past. He has also not behaved in a helpful or constructive way towards himself, although he might be less conscious of this.

In dreaming of the uncle, who is met unexpectedly, the dream is using an image of someone proving to be trustworthy and helpful "unexpectedly". The dream could have used the image of anyone or anything that the person feels is trustworthy and helpful, from a saint to a teacher to their favourite domestic appliance; all these could be associated to being trustworthy and helpful (remember that Hobson describes dreaming as a hyperassociative state), all these figures are similar in relation to their trustworthiness (the unconscious picks out the sameness, what Matte Blanco calls the "symmetry", between the different possible people or things);[2] all these things could, therefore, symbolize helpfulness and trustworthiness. However, by choosing the image of the kindly uncle, the dream conveys a very particular, personal meaning; as Jung put it, "a symbol is the best possible formulation of a relatively unknown psychic content" (Jung 1922, par. 116).

The art of interpreting dreams, therefore, is the art of unlocking the symbol and seeing what the image can represent. As the philosopher Aristotle put it, "The most skilful interpreter of dreams is he who has the faculty of observing resemblances" (Aristotle, 1941, par. 464b, 7–8).

If we take some *stereotypical* examples (and, as I have suggested already, it is important to actually ask the dreamer for their own particular associations to the dream image), we could say that a man in a dream could represent/resemble/be associated with/symbolize the dreamer's father, brother, son, grandfather, uncle, male friend, male part of themselves, male teacher, therapist, or male aspect of their therapist (if the therapist is a woman), or, in fact, anything the dreamer associates with maleness or this man in the dream. You could make a similar list for a woman figure in a dream.

To interpret a dream, therefore, the dreamer and the dream interpreter need simply (!?) to look at the essential qualities of the dream
image; thus, a crocodile might be associated with (symbolize) something primitive, frightening, and voracious; a baby might be associated with vulnerability, dependency, neediness, and interactiveness; a
journey might be associated with change, progression, development,
new experience, and so on and so on.

In this way we can begin to understand the language of the unconscious and symbols and, therefore, the language of dreams.

Notes

1. In defining five characteristics of the unconscious, Freud added timeless-
    ness, absence of mutual contradiction, and replacement of external by
    internal reality (1915e) to his original characteristics of condensation and
    displacement (1900a).
2. Matte Blanco thought that the conscious, rational ego functioned by
    noting the distinctions and differences between one thing and another—
    the asymmetry. For example, the unconscious will help us recognize that
    this animal with four legs and a tail is a horse, as it is similar in a certain
    way to other horses (the unconscious recognizes the symmetry), while
    the ego functions to recognize that this particular horse is Black Beauty
    (it recognizes the asymmetry, the unique difference of this horse from all
    other horses).

CHAPTER FIVE

Unlocking the network of associations: the objective, subjective, transference, and archetypal levels of dreams

I have already touched on the different levels in dreams in previous chapters, but I now look at them in some depth, as it is here that we can see how best to explore and work with the symbolic nature of dreams. Perhaps it is worth stating at the outset, however, that, ultimately, in working with dreams the therapist will ideally move fluidly between these different levels, seeing how the essential symbolic meaning will apply in *any* particular situation and on all levels: on the ordinary, everyday level (objectively), within oneself (subjectively), in the relationship with the therapist (the transference level), and in so far as the dream expresses universal principles, early patterns of relationship, or is particularly powerful or "numinous" (the archetypal level).

In other words, it is not necessary to consciously recognize that you are interpreting a dream on, for example, the subjective or transference levels, this is just a framework that can help think about the different ways that the dream might apply and might, therefore, be thought about. It is helpful to be aware of these different levels, however; if the therapist notices that they rarely look at how the dream applies to the relationship with the therapist (the transference level) they might realize that they are missing a very important and, some would say, vital, facet of the dream. Indeed, there are some schools of thought that treat all dreams that the client has while they are in therapy as relating significantly to the therapeutic relationship, a viewpoint I discuss below.

The objective level . . . and are dreams prophetic?

The objective level is the man-in-the-street's view of dreams, which, in its basic form, treats the dream image as if it corresponds to the actual object in the real world;[1] so, if I dream of meeting my uncle unexpectedly, does this mean that I will *actually* meet him? Or if I dream of my mother dying, does this mean that she will actually die? Or if I dream that I am driving too fast and have a car crash, does it mean that I should take more care and drive more slowly? In this sense, are these dreams prophetic?

There was a time when all dreams were taken to be prophetic and the dreamer would perhaps have consulted some kind of "wise" person to try to offset any bad news they had seen "foretold" by the dream. Jung reports a dream, which appears to be prophetic, which was told him by a man who was a keen mountain climber and who was somewhat arrogant and headstrong. The man joked with Jung, asking him if he was still interpreting dreams and saying he had had "another idiotic dream", and did it mean anything? This was the dream:

> I am climbing a high mountain, over steep snow-covered slopes. I climb higher and higher, and it is marvellous weather. The higher I climb the better I feel. I think, "If only I could go on climbing like this for ever!" When I reach the summit my happiness and elation are so great that I feel I could mount right up into space. And I discover that I can actually do so: I mount upwards on empty air, and awake in sheer ecstasy. [Jung, 1934b, par. 323]

Jung reports that he warned the man about his mountain climbing and strongly urged him to take two guides with him. The man laughed Jung's warning off and, a couple of months later, he was observed to step out into thin air, exactly as he had described to Jung in his dream. He fell onto a young friend who was climbing with him, and both were killed.

So, was the dream truly prophetic? What if someone dreams of driving too fast and having a car crash (not an uncommon dream), does this mean it will happen? The curious thing about Jung's interpretation to the climber is that Jung apparently, and for him uncharacteristically, interpreted his dream entirely on the objective level in an almost non-symbolic manner; in other words, "you have dreamt of a climbing accident so take particular care when you go climbing". I wonder how someone whom Jung describes as headstrong would take to being instructed to "take extra care" when climbing, an instruction that might be experienced as patronizing and which, therefore, might well have been ignored? The dreamer was, in fact, an acquaintance of Jung's rather than a patient, which may account for the fact that Jung did not interpret the dream in his usual way.

Curiously, Jung was, perhaps, conscious of this anomaly, and he gives another, later, account of this dream where he states that he explored the issue further with the dreamer (Jung, 1946, pars 117–123). In this account, Jung says that the dreamer described how the very danger of mountain climbing held a fascination for him and that he thought that death in the mountains would be "something very beautiful". On further discussion, the man alluded to being unhappy in his marriage and with his professional work. When Jung interpreted to him that he thought he was seeking his death in the mountains, the man replied that that was absurd and that, in fact, he was seeking his health there. The end of the story remains the same—some months later he fell to his death.

This later report does take into account inner motives and conflicts and looks at the dream from a more symbolic perspective, even if this was not fully conveyed to the dreamer. If the dreamer's disillusionment with his marriage and career had been interpreted, perhaps the result might have been different . . . but perhaps it is difficult (and maybe even inappropriate) to "interpret" these things to a headstrong acquaintance?

To apply these thoughts to the car crash dream: if someone dreams of driving too fast, I think it is important to treat the dream as symbolic, but recognize that it may *also* apply on the concrete, objective level. The symbolic essence of the dream is that the person is "driving too fast", in other words, taking risks, and not being safe. As I conclude below, the essential question to ask is "where does this symbolic attitude (of driving too fast) apply in this person's life at the present moment?"

There may be many ways in which the dreamer is being rash and taking risks; driving might be one of them. I would suggest that the dreamer needs to attend to their rashness *on all levels*; this would include, perhaps, taking more care with their driving. Paradoxically, if the dream is heeded in this way, it will cease to be prophetic as the "car crash", on whatever level, will be averted.

One could explore one of the most famous prophetic dreams of all in this light—Pharaoh's dream of the seven fat cows which are eaten by seven thin cows. Joseph, who, the Bible reports, interpreted this dream for Pharaoh, took the dream on the objective level, interpreting the cows symbolically. He took the seven fat cows to represent seven years of good harvests, which were followed (eaten up) by seven thin cows, representing seven years of famine. Pharaoh accepted this interpretation and duly put aside extra grain during the seven years of good harvests and, when the seven years of famine did, in fact, follow, the country was able to weather this difficult time due to Joseph's interpretation of the dream.

Whether or not the psyche is able to see into the future (a question to which I do not have the answer!), I think it is certainly the case, as described in Chapter Four, that the psyche is all the time picking up on myriad pieces of information. As the ruler of Egypt, Pharaoh would have been subtly tuned in to everything related to his country (if he was a good ruler). It is possible that he would have been able to unconsciously discern patterns relating to harvests, civil unrest, or political danger that would have emerged in the form of dreams. One of the prime roles of the unconscious, and of dreaming in particular, is to decode, process, and make sense of this information. After all, it is the patterns that are operative in us, and the world around us, which determine what we do and how we will act; the future is, in this respect, already partially written.

One could justifiably ask at this point why, if this information is so important, it is not clearer and easier to understand. To which the answer is that dreams and dream images simply reflect the way the unconscious works and processes things, and that when this functioning is understood it is not so difficult to understand the meaning of dreams.

With regard to dreams being prophetic, Aristotle reached a similar conclusion over 2000 years ago. He did not think that dreams were prophetic;[2] instead, he thought that dreams could be used, in particular, to diagnose bodily illnesses as he thought we were more sensitive to the images and sense impressions at night and the dreamer could, thus, pick up what is going on in the body and elsewhere (Aristotle, 1941, par. 464).

Jung deals with this point by describing the "prospective" (forward-looking) function of dreams, writing,

> it would be wrong to call [dreams] prophetic, because at bottom they are no more prophetic than a medical diagnosis or a weather forecast. They are merely an anticipatory combination of probabilities which may coincide with the actual behaviour of things but need not necessarily agree in every detail. Only in the latter case can we speak of "prophecy". That the prospective function of dreams is sometimes greatly superior to the combinations we can consciously foresee is not surprising, since a dream results from the fusion of subliminal elements and is thus a combination of all the perceptions, thoughts and feelings which consciousness has not registered because of their feeble accentuation. [Jung, 1948[1916], par. 493]

Having briefly explored the question of prophetic dreams, I conclude the discussion of dreams on the objective level with two observations/thoughts. Peters (1990) gives the example of a person who dreams of someone they met for the first time that day whom they consciously liked, yet that night they dream that the person is a thief. Peters suggests the dreamer has picked up something untrustworthy about the person, but they are not conscious of it and it is, therefore, expressed in a dream.[3] In this case the dream image might apply primarily to the actual person dreamt about, and their being a thief might refer, symbolically, to some kind of dishonesty or other, perhaps even to their being an actual thief.

Jung tells the story of Sophocles, the ancient Greek poet, who "did not believe in dreams" but who dreamt repeatedly that a certain man had stolen a precious vessel from the temple of Hermes and hidden it in a certain place. He ignored the dream at first, but when he dreamt it a second and a third time he eventually disclosed his dream, and the vessel was duly found where Sophocles had dreamt it was (Jung, 1984[1938], p. 5).

Sometimes, then, the dream images could apply realistically to individuals or situations as they are in real life; however, it is always wise to treat dream images as symbols and recognize that these symbols might *also* apply to the actual people or situations as depicted in the dream, *viz.* the mountain climbing and car crash dreams.

That such concrete, objective dreams are relatively rare is not to suggest that the dream world is not engaged with the dreamer's actual situation in the "real world", quite the reverse, in fact. Blechner, in his excellent book on dreams (2001), points out that if the therapist actively asks the dreamer whether they can connect a dream to an actual situation, then the dreamer can usually do so in a high percentage of cases—he suggests as high as 92%. Blechner points out that the therapist has to actively question the dreamer in this way to elicit the connection, otherwise dreamers will much less frequently make the connection to actual events or situations; he suggests the frequency of connection drops to only 38% (Palombo, 1984, quoted in Blechner, 2001 p. 57).

Blechner gives the example of a client who dreamt as follows:

> She was a burglar and she was burgling a business building downtown. The building had a marble lobby, brass elevators and a guard. The dreamer had an accomplice, a man of her age, she didn't know who it was. She said the dream had a teenage quality. The money was in the basement, she went down after midnight and climbed down the elevator shaft. She took the money and put it in her pocket and wasn't caught. She returned the next day to try to improve her technique, she had a flashlight so that she wouldn't have to turn on the light. She took some more money but the next day she went again to the building but the guard noticed her and suspected her. [Blechner, 2001, pp. 54–55]

Blechner reports that his client herself suggested three different interpretations for the dream: that she was feeling guilty about having increased the number of sessions she was attending and that perhaps she felt she was stealing money from her husband; a sexual interpretation relating to the torch and descending into the lift shaft, which she linked with masturbation; and something shameful linked to the building in the dream where, in fact, her "professional technique" had been exposed.

Blechner said that all these interpretations seemed valid, yet he was struck by the burglary aspect of the dream, and he asked her if she had ever committed a burglary. She described two instances from her teenage years. The next session, however, she looked embarrassed and confessed that the previous year he had made an error with her bill and had assumed she had paid for a month that she had not, in fact, paid for. She said she now realized that this was the burglary in the dream (Blechner works in a similar building to that of the dream), and she duly gave him a cheque for the month for which she had not paid.

This corresponds with the findings of dream researchers critical of the Freudian dream disguise model, who have collected many thousands of dreams. Their conclusion is that dreams can be clearly seen to relate to the waking concerns of the dreamer and often, while the dream material might be in a "novel construction", it is frequently not difficult to see to what it refers (Domhoff, 2004).

One of the prime considerations in interpreting a dream, therefore (and one of the questions I frequently ask when someone tells me a dream), is: "is there anything in your current life to which this might apply?"

In regard to the dream of unexpectedly meeting your uncle, it is possible that this event might actually occur, but to conclude that that is the central meaning of the dream is to close down on much else. Similarly, while one might consider whether a dream of your mother dying might apply on the objective level (has she been ill? Is the dream alerting you to something you have not noticed?), such dreams are more often found to apply primarily on the subjective level, which we now come to. On this level, the "death" can be treated symbolically as relating to something of the way your mother is, or the way you related to your mother, that has been internalized and has become a part of the dreamer. The dream might symbolize that it is this mother-like way-of-being that is dying off and changing.

The subjective level

It is interpretations on the subjective level that are perhaps most associated with Jung. As he put it, interpretation on the subjective level "refers every part of the dream and all the actors in it back to the dreamer himself" (Jung, 1917, par. 130).[4] In this way, the death of mother can refer to an internal change and, as I outlined in earlier chapters, meeting an uncle unexpectedly can refer to the dreamer unexpectedly discovering the helpful, supportive, avuncular qualities in and towards themselves.

In an essay that I thoroughly recommend (Jung, 1917), Jung interpreted the following dream of one of his patients:

> She is about to cross a wide river. There is no bridge, but she finds a ford where she can cross. She is on the point of doing so, when a large crab that lay hidden in the water seizes her by the foot and will not let her go. She wakes up in terror.

His patient associated the river with a boundary that is difficult to cross; she said she thought it related to the fact that she was progressing slowly in therapy. She associated the ford to an opportunity to cross in safety, and said that perhaps the therapy was offering her a way of surmounting the obstacle she needed to overcome. She associated the crab, which is hidden in the water, with cancer (in German, the word for cancer (the disease), crab, and the zodiacal sign of cancer are the same—*Krebs*); she said that the disease had killed a spontaneous, creative, impulsive, acquaintance of hers. She associated the whole dream to her relationship with a friend, which she felt was holding her back.

Jung first interprets the dream on the objective level, suggesting that this would correspond to a "Freudian" interpretation of the dream. An interpretation on this level would suggest that the dreamer knows she ought to cross the river, that is, give up relations with her friend, but that she would much rather her friend does not let her out of her embraces (the grip of the crab); this represents "an infantile wish" not to change and, as a result, she is "pulled back into the river" and cannot proceed or progress.

However, Jung goes on to elaborate the dream further on the subjective level, suggesting that the river, the crab, and all the elements in the dream represent elements within the dreamer herself. In particular, he explored with his patient her associations to the crab, to cancer, and to her acquaintance who had died of the disease. It turned out that the woman who had died had, in fact, had an affair with an artist. When she had contracted cancer and died the dreamer had seen this as some kind of punishment meted out due to her impulsiveness and the affair.

Jung proposed, therefore, that it was the dreamer's own spontaneity, creativity, and "masculine" features that were represented by the crab and, in particular, the patient's foot, which the crab seizes. He suggested that it was these parts of the dreamer that she did not want to recognize and embrace, as the dreamer feared that they were dangerous, and that she was, thus, held by the crab in the water, unable to cross/progress. The dreamer's attachment to her friend was, thus, determined by her attitude to herself and, in particular, to certain aspects of herself that she had not accepted and integrated.

The transference level

Jung made this interpretation to his patient but found that she did not recognize herself as spontaneous, creative, or "masculine", but that, rather, she saw herself as fragile, sensitive, and feminine. For her, Jung's interpretation did not fit. He wondered why this was and where the "power" that had previously been experienced in relation to the woman who died of cancer was now located. Therefore, he asked his patient how she saw him. She replied that when she was with him he seemed pleasant, but when she was not with him he appeared rather "dangerous and sinister, like an evil magician or a demon" (*ibid.*, par. 143).

Jung concluded that, in carrying this projection, he had become the obstacle, the crab, which prevented her crossing the river and making progress. In interpreting this to his patient, something changed. She said he had touched on a horrible feeling she had about her friend, "something inhuman, evil and cruel". Jung felt that, in recognizing this, his patient had "entered a new phase of life without knowing it".

It is this kind of experience that makes psychotherapeutic work so effective; the client and therapist are not simply talking about something on a theoretical level: rather, the client can experience the issue in relationship to the therapist and in the immediacy and security of the therapeutic relationship.

Looking at the transference level of dreams is, therefore, particularly important and illuminating. In this vein, I suggested that the dream of meeting one's uncle unexpectedly might have been primarily concerned with the client's experience with their therapist, whom they were finding unexpectedly helpful and "avuncular".

It can be argued that almost all dreams that are dreamt in the span of a therapy, as well as some dreamt before and after, either refer directly to the relationship with the therapist or can be seen to also apply to, and to have consequences for, the therapeutic relationship. This accords with the Kleinian view that all the client's comments, free associations, dreams, etc. can be understood to relate on this level (Joseph, 1985). If all dreams are applied only or primarily to the relationship to the therapist, it is possible that this might feel claustrophobic to the client, as if the therapist is self-centred and relates everything to him/herself, but it is very important to include the transference perspective.

As Cambray and Carter (2004, p. 130) and Wilkinson point out, dreams emerge in the context of the containing, therapeutic relationship and, particularly concerning work with early relational trauma, it is this relationship that may make it possible to "dream the undreamable as a prelude to becoming able to think the unthinkable" (Wilkinson, 2006, p. 148). The dream can be an important step in becoming able to live with traumatic experience and modify relational patterns. I shall give other examples of transference level interpretations later.

Blechner points out that dreams about the therapist and the therapy also serve as supervision for the therapist, enabling the therapist to reflect on their role in the therapy and how the client sees them. He gives the following example:

> A client dreamt that he was sitting across from his therapist at a restaurant and could not understand what he was saying.

While much else could be gleaned from this dream, for example, concerning the "food" and the nature of the restaurant, Blechner reports that the therapist reported this dream at a conference and that many of those in the audience could not understand what he was saying either (Blechner, 2001, p. 212). Perhaps the dream was trying to communicate the client's very real difficulty in understanding the therapist. Although this dream realistically portrays the therapist, exploring the transference level of dreams as described above also serves as a constant form of feedback about the process of the therapy and, thus, as supervision for the therapist (see further example in Chapter Eight).

The archetypal level

The word archetypal has a range of meanings, from universal, common to all, and typical, to significant, powerful, and awe-inspiring, as

well as primitive, unformed, and early. The archetypal level illuminates particular dream images, patterns, themes, and stories with
reference to powerful general patterns that frequently relate to early
experience in some way (I shall look particularly at the significance of
early experience in the next chapter). The archetypal level of dreams
might be experienced, therefore, as subjectively more powerful and
significant and might also touch on important universal themes: for
example, Jung's dream of the house with the different floors describes
some universal truths about the psyche.

Jung suggests that the fact that in the crab dream the dreamer was
bitten on the foot was significant. The dreamer had large "masculine"
feet and she plays the "masculine" role with her friend.[5] The foot is
"typically" the part of all of us that meets the hard earth of reality: we
have to "take the next step" in order to progress, to "put one foot in
front of the other", to put our "best foot forward", or we can be "on
the back foot" if we are struggling. In this dream, the foot is sensitive
and exposed and is bitten by the crab, indicating perhaps that the
dreamer is taking a risk and exposing something sensitive in trying to
progress.

Jung suggests that the foot symbolizes masculinity and suggests
that it often has phallic significance. He comes to this conclusion, in
part, with reference to the myths of Osiris and Isis, and Oedipus. In
the myth, Osiris is dismembered by the god of the underworld, Set;
Isis collects together the pieces of Osiris's body, although she cannot
find the phallus, which has been eaten by the fishes. Isis and Osiris's
phantom "lie together" and their offspring is Harpocrates (also known
as Horus), who is weak and deformed in the lower limbs—the feet
(Jung, 1911–1912, par. 356). Hence, a link is made between the feet,
masculinity, and phallic potency. Similarly, in the Oedipus myth,
Oedipus, who has one swollen foot (the name Oedipus actually means
"swell-foot") meets a man on the road whom he kills, who, he discovers later, is his natural father. He then continues his journey and
ends up marrying a woman who, unbeknown to him, is his mother,
as he had been adopted at birth in order to prevent this very occur-
rence, which had been foretold. Both myths link the foot with phallic
power.

One could suggest that in the crab dream, the dreamer has Oedipal
difficulties as she is not able to claim her creativity and masculinity
and progress as she is afraid of its murderous/destructive elements,

which she saw in the woman's affair with the artist and which the dreamer felt was punished by her death from cancer; in other words, she has repressed this side of herself. This is a Freudian type of interpretation—the repression of "masculine" sexual desire and potency, which is parallel to Jung's interpretation. The difference is that, for Jung, the woman's masculinity and creativity have been projected onto others and not claimed for herself, while for Freud, it is the forbidden wish that is repressed. Perhaps the interpretations are not so different after all.

In looking at the archetypal level of the dream, the dream interpreter is trying to discover the symbolic essence of the dream and dream images; he/she is trying to discover whether a particular dream image has a universal significance and meaning or whether personal associations are more relevant; usually, the therapist tries to blend both personal and universal aspects.

For example, Jung's dream of the house with the different floors is archetypal to the extent that everyone's psyche might be thought to be made up of parts that are conscious and other parts which are more inaccessible and unconscious. For this reason, a dream of a house is often taken to symbolize the individual's own psyche (unless there are good reasons to think otherwise)—it is "where the person lives". The personal aspects relate to the particular nature of the house in the dream, which will show the particular characteristics of the individual's psyche that are relevant at the time of the dream.

The same is true of any image. For example, a dream image of a dog may be thought to archetypally (typically) relate to a figure that is faithful and loyal, "man's best friend". In addition, however, we would need to look at the particular nature of the dog in the dream and to the dreamer's personal associations to dogs and to this dog in particular. If it is a fierce dog, it might relate to something of which the dreamer is afraid, possibly a vicious part of their nature; the three-headed dog, Cerberus, was said to guard the path to Hades (the underworld)—could that be relevant? The British Prime Minister, Winston Churchill, called his depression his "black dog", referring, presumably, to his depression's dark, oppressive nature and the way it followed him around. If the dreamer was once bitten by a dog, the dream image will carry that personal meaning as something more or less threatening to the dreamer. One aspect of the art of dream interpretation is to be able to blend these different elements together into a coherent narrative that illuminates the individual's current situation.

The numinous quality of archetypal dreams

Sometimes, dreams have a larger-than-life quality, a sense of something spiritual, magical, or mysterious about them. Jung called this sense "numinous", while Freud referred to it as "oceanic". This can be another aspect of these powerful and important archetypal dreams. For example, a client had the following dream at a particularly significant moment in her therapy:

I am having my psychotherapy session in a small building opposite the main part of my parents' house—it is a classroom. I am on the couch as normal, with you sitting on my left, but you tell me it is too hot in the room and that we should continue the session outside. You have put some chairs in the courtyard. I register my annoyance with you for this as it interrupts the session; although I recognize that it is hot, I think it is not hot enough to need to be outside. Outside in the courtyard, I recognize the chairs you've set up are from the dining area of my kitchen. I notice that you are taking your clothes off and also that a young boy, aged 8–9 is playing on his own.

As we sit down to proceed with the session, we all notice that it is getting darker and that the atmosphere has changed. You step away from the chairs to see what is happening. I make a step closer to you and together we look up to see that the sky has opened up to reveal the solar system and all the planets, like in a planetarium. All comes to a standstill as the solar system reveals itself in slow motion, lit by the moon. One after the other the planets are revealed, except for the sun. The scene is immense, magical, real, magnificent—a transcendent moment. You and I, standing next to each other, witness and experience this moment mesmerised.

We are interrupted by the little boy, who calls my name in a panic. He tells me that my house is being attacked and points towards it. My house (in the dream) is the veranda of my parents' house (which was where the family spent a lot of time, related to which I have a lot of traumatic memories). I look to my house to see people trashing it mercilessly. Without moving, I take a deep breath and I blow across into my house. I am surprised at the power of my blow when I realize that it has wiped out and destroyed the people trashing my house. I also notice that my blow has divided the veranda—my house—to give me two rooms. The rooms are now new and are furnished to a very high standard. The furnishing, however, is old-fashioned, a vintage style, which at first I am not entirely sure about but very quickly come to like and appreciate. Still standing next to you, I look at my new rooms and admire the combination of modern colours, painted walls, and vintage furniture. We return to the chairs to proceed with our session. I notice that you are fully dressed now but that my upper body is naked. I feel fine with this as I have no urge to cover myself up; you are not shocked to see me naked either. We sit down and proceed with the session.

I will not be able to cover all elements of this dream, but the outline understanding that the dreamer and I reached together, working from her associations, is as follows. The dream, which is clearly based in a transference setting, since the scene is related primarily to a therapy session, also has powerful, numinous elements—the awe-inspiring vision of the solar system. To some extent, the dream offers an overview of the therapy itself, which has served to provide "therapy" for, and a "classroom" learning experience about, the dreamer's frequently traumatic early life.

The dreamer registers that she is annoyed with me for shifting the site of the therapy to outside in the courtyard. In fact, the focus of the therapy itself did shift from an initial "hot house" emphasis on the relationship between us to more open, universal themes relating to her deeper self (in the Jungian sense of the word): the courtyard could be seen as a symbol of the self, as Jung often interpreted squares to relate to the self, through the coming together of the four functions of the personality.[6] In practice, this shift partly occurred through my under-standing and interpreting some of her positive, erotic/sexual feeling towards me (the hot house) primarily as an element of her wish to relate, to be appreciated, and to bring forward some of the parts of her self and her life force/libido which she had not been able to express in her childhood.

In the dream, she recognizes that the chairs are from her dining room/kitchen. They are, therefore, associated with food and eating; in other words, something good and nourishing is available here. She notices I am taking my clothes off, relating, perhaps, to the personal, human, direct nature of our work together. The young boy in the dream, a figure that has appeared in other dreams, symbolizes the developing part of her that is playfully and inquisitively exploring and learning about herself and the world through therapy.

The atmosphere changes and darkens as we go deeper into what had previously been unconscious forms of functioning, and an awe-inspiring vision of the solar system appears. The solar system could be understood to be another symbol of the self and the different forces within the self—the planets have been taken to symbolize archetypal forces for millennia, as represented, for example, in astrological symbolism. In the therapy, she was able to connect up with herself in a profound way and come to see things much more clearly: personal, relational, and social dynamics. She was also able to appreciate the beauty and reality of the forces "out there"; the solar system inspires awe, and observing it in this way reminds us of our relatively small place within it. She was able to observe these forces, but did not over-identify with them, so that they remained "out there" in their proper place; over-identifying with the power of the unconscious self can, at worst, lead to psychosis (although the next scene shows us that she has been able to draw on some measure of personal power). The dream three times emphasizes that this occurred while standing "close to you"/"next to each other", in other words, the containment of the therapy and the relationship with me are important in this.

It is significant that the planets are revealed through the light of the moon, which traditionally, archetypally, is associated with "the feminine", feeling, the unconscious, and change (this only scratches the surface of the deep symbolism of the moon). The client very much "feels her way" in any particular situation, picking up unconscious cues from those around her. In her life, this deeper, sensitive, feeling approach (rather than, say, a more overtly powerful, conscious, domineering, "solar" approach) has meant that she has sometimes been exploited, used, and undervalued. The result of this is symbolized, perhaps, by her house being "trashed". Through the therapy she has gained confidence in her own power, the power of her feelings, and her power to express herself (the power of "breath"). In the dream, she uses this to blow away the attackers, just as she has become able to argue forcefully both to defend herself and to create and obtain what she wants—the rooms are transformed in the house.

The fact that there are two rooms suggests that a helpful division has developed, reflected in her increasing ability to reflect upon, contain, and make good use of her feelings—one room for thinking (ego-functioning) and one for feeling (her core self). This has come about to some extent through the therapy, which seemed to her at first "old-fashioned, a vintage style" that she was "not entirely sure about" but which she "very quickly [came] to like and appreciate". She has now created her own new, "modern", personal space through combining these elements.

When we return to the chairs to continue our work, she notices that I am dressed but that she is half-naked; she recognizes, perhaps, the value of the professional, "clothed" therapy, while feeling comfortable about showing and sharing her core, "half-naked" self with me. The dream came at a significant point in her therapy, indicating, among other things, that while her core self had been comfortably laid bare in the therapy (the planets and her nakedness are revealed), it remained for her to find suitable ways of clothing this inner self, so that she could function in the outer, "solar", daytime world of work and professional relationships in a less exposed and more manageable way.

The powerful, transcendent, archetypal nature of the dream reflects the profundity of the dreamer's experience of, and contact with, her core self and the world around her at that moment, as well as of the power and importance of the insights and themes that the dream conveys.

Amplification

In discussing the archetypal nature of dreams, I have mentioned the myths of Osiris and Isis, and Oedipus, and the figures of Cerberus and Winston Churchill. This is because archetypal patterns, relating to universal experience, are often best identified and exemplified in myths, legends, and fairytales, as well as in film, television, or through other cultural or iconic stories or figures. Jung called the process of exploring and expanding on the meaning of a particular dream image with reference to archetypal material "amplification", in other words, the images and themes are amplified, in the sense of made larger and clearer.

I am deviating from Jung's classical understanding of archetypes here in including the generalized *cultural* influences on the individual—what has been called the cultural unconscious (Adams, 2001;

Henderson, 1988). These influences are not universal across all civilizations, but refer to influences that will be general to the particular culture in which the dreamer was raised and in which they have lived. These cultural influences will include national, local, religious, ethnic, and family elements.

Someone brought up as a Catholic in the UK will have been immersed in a different cultural milieu from someone brought up as a Hindu in India; this will be reflected in the different meanings that particular dream images may symbolize. At its simplest, my unconscious may symbolize a certain characteristic, for example, bravery, by using the image of a particular figure from a film or a soap opera, which might well be unknown to someone from a different culture.

It is important, therefore, to take extra care when working with people from other cultures to explore the matrix of meaning around particular dream images for them. For example, one client dreamt of a child being captured by Zulus; it was important that we explored what characteristics and associations she had to Zulus, coming, as she did, from a related culture. This underlines good practice in every case, as one of the most common errors in dream analysis is to assume we know what a particular image may mean without eliciting the dreamer's associations and amplifications.

The archetypal figures and patterns, for example, of the hero, the shadow, betrayal, jealousy, love, hate, rivalry, and so on, are likely to be depicted in a "modern idiom", with dreams of the hero symbolized by current statesmen, rebels, or characters or stories from films, books, or television. This does not make them any less archetypal, as the essential characteristics are the same whether we are looking at the classical myth of Odysseus or the more modern "myth" of Luke Skywalker in the *Star Wars* films.

In the next chapter, I explore how these different levels and techniques are used in beginning to work with a dream that the client brings.

Notes

1. "I call every interpretation which equates the dream images with real objects an interpretation on the objective level" (Jung, 1917, par. 130).

2. Nor did he think they were "messages from God", as he thought that as even "the lower animals" and "common people" dream, then, he concluded, God would not be sending them messages—a highly dubious piece of logic.

3. Jung (1948[1945], par. 542) gives a similar example of a man who had repeated disturbing dreams that his new fiancée, who was from "a good family", was behaving in sexually inappropriate ways. At Jung's suggestion, he investigated the matter and discovered that it was, in fact, the case (he broke off the engagement).

4. Elsewhere he writes, "a dream is a theatre in which the dreamer is himself the scene, the player, the prompter, the producer, the author, the public and the critic . . . all figures in the dream [are] personified features of the dreamer's own personality" (Jung, 1948[1916], par. 509).

5. These stereotypically "masculine" roles can equally well be adopted by men and women.

6. Thinking, feeling, intuition, and sensation (Jung, 1921).

CHAPTER SIX

Beginning work with a dream

"So difficult is it to understand a dream that for a long time I have made it a rule, when someone tells me a dream and asks for my opinion, to say first of all to myself: "I have no idea what this dream means". After that I can begin to examine the dream"

(Jung, 1948[1945], par. 533)

A young man, well established in therapy, brings the following dream:

A young woman, "A", is lurking behind her horse for surprise, she runs out, grabs her metal spike weapon and attacks another young woman, "B". I admire the attack. The first time she has no success, but the second time she kills "B" by giving her a bear hug which breaks her neck. I move to go and help, but don't as I'm too afraid to lose my life.

The first thing to ask with any dream is what associations the dreamer has to the dream. Exploring the dream in this way is the most important aspect of working on a dream.[1] I usually ask this in a general way, and note which parts of the dream the dreamer associates to first. As this is a dream about known characters, it is important to find out what characteristics these individuals have in real life.

The dreamer tells me that he knows A through his current work: she is flirty, dozy, lazy, but very winning; in the dream she is wearing black; he knows B from a past connection, she was very successful, although she had a sister who was at times self-destructive; in the dream she is wearing white. He said the weapon was very nasty and that A was twirling it around viciously.

Something about these figures in the dream, and particularly the hug, make me begin to think of the client's struggle to form a success-ful relationship, which is one of the core themes of the therapy. I have noticed before that he appears to undermine potential relationships in some way that we have not properly understood yet. I wonder if this dream, which somehow "seems important" (although I could not quite say why at this point), might be telling us something about this.

I notice that he has not said anything about the horse in the dream and I ask him about that. He says that nothing occurs to him about it except that it is black.

I wonder to myself what this black horse might symbolize, and think that a horse is a powerful animal that might be more or less well controlled. I think of the centaur that is half man half horse, and that horses traditionally carried people (in the way that one's body "carries" the individual). I hypothesize that the horse might, therefore, represent the body and, for this young man, his bodily and sexual desire.[2]

I wonder if the fact that the horse is black symbolizes these urges, which he regards as "dark" (the theme of dark/light–good/bad is reinforced by the fact that A is wearing black and B is wearing white in the dream). As he has no particular personal associations to this horse, I feel more confident to interpret the horse on this archetypal level; in other words, my associations to the black horse represent my amplification of the horse image with reference to the archetypal level.

The client has finished describing his associations to the dream, and I ask him if he has any thoughts about what this dream might refer to. This young man quite often brings dreams and sometimes has a sense of what they might mean or where they might apply. His initial thoughts have often proved insightful and, even if the interpretations I have brought have led in another direction, the different ideas usually complement each other. On this occasion, he says he can make little of the dream.

I ask him what the feeling is in the dream. He says that when he woke up he felt enormous pain and fear.

As I listen to him telling the dream and to his associations, a sense of a possible meaning forms in my mind. I have collected enough associations to the dream in this vital first stage of the process and I am now ready to engage with the dream and the dreamer.[3] While I have a sense of a possible meaning, I am not yet clear about all the details. I treat this initial sense very much as a hypothesis that has to be tested. Most important in the testing is to see whether it rings true with the dreamer, and whether the details will fall into place.

I will often (usually) begin interpreting a dream before I have worked out the details; the dreamer will often themselves elaborate on the interpretation, noting links I have missed, adding other associations which either fit or add extra information that I had not seen or which had not been obvious in the initial telling of the dream. Sometimes, the dreamer will remember extra bits of the dream. I am hoping to achieve a state where the dreamer and I are working together on the dream as this tends to be the most fruitful way of interpreting dreams, although, obviously, the personality of the dreamer will play a part in this; by which I mean, whether someone expects me to do the work in interpreting the dream, or whether they "get in first", offering already formulated interpretations of their own. These ways of using dreams and relating to the therapist are things that I would pick up and explore with the client over time.

On this occasion, I begin by saying that I am struck by the hug in the dream, and that I wonder if the dream might be about what happens in the relationships that he is struggling with. Note that I say, "I wonder if . . .", which conveys my sense that my understanding and interpretation is provisional, a hypothesis (as Jung said, "every interpretation is a hypothesis" (Jung, 1934b, p. 322)). I do not expect myself to "know" the meaning of a dream and I would be concerned if I thought I did "know" the meaning before any discussion with the dreamer, although sometimes I might have more conviction and feel confident in my sense of the dream, while at other times I am much more tentative and uncertain.

I suggest that the girl who runs out from behind the horse might symbolize the part of him (which is different from his conscious personality and attitude) that approaches relationships aggressively, wanting sexual gratification, as she is wielding a metal spike (penis, weapon). I suggest that he "admires" this kind of approach (as he says in the dream), feeling that such a sexually aggressive approach to women might be good (a compensation, as Jung would call it, for consciously not feeling powerful and potent perhaps); I suggest that perhaps that kind of approach would be "flirty, lazy, dozy, and winning" (the characteristics he has ascribed to A)—in other words, not a straightforward approach.

I continue with the interpretation, following the narrative of the dream, saying that the first time he has "no success", he does not "penetrate her with his spike"; in other words, this way does not lead to (sexual) satisfaction. His other approach is through his need—a bear hug—but that kills her. His need is the greater threat as it is so overwhelming. Perhaps, on the objective level (in reality), the women he approaches pick up the neediness beneath his overt sexuality and this undermines the relationship.

He is clearly interested in this interpretation and we discuss B together. She is desirable, successful, and good (she went to a prestigious university); is this just what is desirable to him, or do we need to look at the dream on another level, too? We also note that there is another aspect of B, represented by her sister, who is troubled and sometimes self-destructive; on the objective level, he is attracted to women who are vulnerable and have a darker side, or, again, perhaps this can be understood on another level (see below).

In the dream, he "moves to go and help but then doesn't because he's too afraid to lose his life". So, he is keeping his distance from this conflict for some reason: perhaps he is afraid to lose the "life" given to him by the aggressive part and, although he recognizes that there is a problem, he does not do anything about it. Something is stopping him from addressing his (sexually) aggressive and needy reactions to relationships. At this point the discussion of the dream branches out in different directions, with the dreamer taking up the points I have made. This, therefore, feels to me that the interpretation has struck a chord, since the dreamer has engaged with the interpretation and it has led us on to discussing new things.

The subjective level of the dream

If we look at the dream on the subjective level, we would interpret all the figures in the dream as part of the dreamer: the dreamer's dream-ego (the ego is the part he most identifies with) being the "I" in the dream, with A symbolizing the sexually aggressive part, associated with his pent-up bodily needs (the horse), and B symbolizing his more successful part, which has been able to achieve success at work, although this part of him has a shadow side (the self-destructive sister), which he is aware could cause him trouble in practical ways.

We could interpret this as the threat to the successful, socially well-orientated (ego) part of himself from his needy, sexual feelings, which threaten to overwhelm him at times. In the dream, B's neck is broken; I did not ask for associations about the neck but, archetypally, the neck is what links one's thinking (head) to one's feelings (body): if the neck is broken, there is a traumatic (fatal) dislocation between feeling and thinking. He has learnt to deal with his more overt sexual behaviour—the attack with the spike—but his neediness—the hug—is actually the greater threat. He rather admires the sexually aggressive part (he admires the attack in the dream); perhaps it makes him feel potent and, although he wants to help in the dream, he does not actually do so; yet the dream is alerting him to the threat from these two parts of himself and the conflict between them.

He says he feels pain and fear in the dream and on waking from the dream. These are two feelings that are familiar to him: the pain relates to his sense of emptiness and loneliness at not having a relationship, the fear relates to his concern that his unsatisfied desires will lead him to do something that will damage him. The fact that he frequently talks about these feelings in relation to these issues reinforces the thought that the dream does refer to these things.

The transference level of the dream

The therapy with me was almost "killed off" at our first meeting, as the dreamer did not want to agree to give me the four weeks' notice that I ask for when it comes to ending therapy. This required some careful discussion and negotiation between us. We discussed this in terms of whether agreeing to give me four weeks' notice at that point would be giving me undue power, as well as making him feel needy and attacked/dominated by me.

In terms of the dream, we could see this as relating to a needy, powerful, sexually potent/aggressive part of him (A) attacking the thinking "successful" figure (B), me, and/or, in reverse, me as a needy, greedy, sexually aggressive and powerful therapist (A) exercising my power over him and killing him (B) off. This describes the archetypal pattern involved, the way that bodily feeling and sexual desire can overpower thinking and socially adapted ego-functioning, and that unrequited need can lead to behaviour that does not fit well with constructive functioning.

By this stage in the therapy, however, we have moved on a good deal and the therapy is well established. We could see that he might feel that his neediness and wish to dominate might kill off our relationship and he wants to keep away from that (this may have sexual aspects). This may also represent a wish to "beat me" by overpowering my "intellectual" interpretations (B was well educated) with his powerful bodily urges, proving my interpretations ineffectual against the power of his emotions and desires, but he recognizes that that would be self-defeating.

We could also speculate that his needs (the hug) might be the thing that might actually kill off the relationship, for example, his concern about money in the first session, or his personal needs that I cannot satisfy and which might, therefore, make him feel that the therapy would ultimately be a failure.

A return to the objective level via the archetypal level

There is a way that the archetypal level also links back to the objective level, since archetypal patterns embody and describe patterns of relationship that were laid down in the individual's early life. Such early patterns of relating between the infant and their early care-givers are what Daniel Stern calls "ways-of-being-with-others" (Stern, 1985); John Bowlby, from a slightly different frame of reference, calls them attachment patterns (Bowlby, 1969, 1980). These archetypal patterns, as reflected in dreams, are often describing patterns of early experience from the dreamer's life.

Jung's theory was that, for the child, these archetypal, by which I mean, here, powerful general patterns, become "humanized" and made more bearable by actual experience in the world. The archetypes have two poles: the very best and the very worst kinds of experience, for example, the archetypal "Great Mother" can be experienced as wonderfully giving and benevolent or terrifyingly depriving and attacking. According to Jung, someone who has not had sufficient ordinary, good experience with their mother might remain longing for an idealized loving experience with their mother, or a mother substitute, and dread a terrifying, annihilating experience.[4]

In his early life, the dreamer's mother was diagnosed with a serious illness and had to undergo invasive surgery. As a result, she was physically and emotionally unavailable for quite long periods of his childhood. One of his poignant memories was that due to her inconsistency and unavailability, he had often rejected her and she had, perhaps, at times given up trying to reconnect with him. In this way, she had been the one who had experienced the rejection (he had projected his experience of rejection into her), since he had turned away from her as he could not bear the uncertainty and frustration.

We might understand the dream as the dreamer's unsuccessful attempt to get through to his mother at first (he could not penetrate her with his spike; he felt powerless) and then that his need (the hug) killed her off as he rejected her; the hug was killing rather than satisfying. It was safer for him to be in control of the rejection, better for him to kill off rather than be killed. From the therapy, we are aware that he wants to be in control in important relationships where he might experience comfort, satisfaction, or excitement and where he might, therefore, be vulnerable: for example, because he could lose what he so values.

We might speculate that the reason that he cannot do anything about the attack in the dream, even though he wants to help, is that this pattern is part of his natural way of relating and that he cannot simply "change it" (it is held in what is called implicit memory (see Knox 2003)). It will be through the process of therapy, through making these patterns conscious and seeing how they manifest themselves in the transference relationship, that the patterns can gradually lose their power and their determining grip and be supplemented by more satisfying and fulfilling ways of relating.

The "life" that he is afraid to lose in the dream might come from the life given through this primary, early form of relating, which, therefore, connects him with his core self and other people, rather than the "liveliness" of aggression *per se*.

As Blechner states, the dream can be seen to refer back to actual experiences in the world, in other words, to experiences on the objective level. They are so far back, however, and so much a part of the dreamer's formative experiences, that they relate more to patterns of relationship rather than single experiences. Such patterns of relationship usually develop after a repeated kind of experience, for example, the dreamer repeatedly trying to get through to his mother but finding her unavailable. These patterns are, thus, archetypally powerful for the dreamer and will have had a powerful influence on his life. Dreams are particularly good at elucidating these early patterns of relationship, which are held in implicit memory, that are otherwise difficult to come to know about.

In fact, we did not take up these aspects of either the transference relationship or the archetypal elements in our first discussion of the dream, although we can see that these meanings are "present" in the dream. We have, however, explored these aspects of the dreamer and his relationship to me in other ways, in respect to other dreams, and in returning to discuss this dream further. Often, there is simply too much in one dream to explore fully at first, and the dream is taken up largely on one particular level. In this case, initially, we took it up mostly on the objective and subjective levels, with reference to his real-world relationships and the inner conflicts between his needs and desires, as I have described. (See Chapter Ten for a discussion of an initial dream that was returned to many times over the course of a therapy and was explored thoroughly on every level.)

I hope I have given a sense of how one might go about interpreting a dream. Clearly, every therapist will develop their own style of approaching a dream, and, ideally, this will change and evolve over time and will probably be different with each dreamer and with each dream, depending on what is going on in the therapy at that particular moment. I shall now, in the next chapter, make a few observations about the essentials of dream interpretation.

Notes

1. Jung sees this exploration of the dreamer's own associations as central to the process of understanding a dream; he calls it "taking up the context"

(Jung, 1948[1945], par. 542). Colman (2010) also emphasizes the importance of the network of associations in the creation of symbolic meaning in dreams.

2. Jung suggests that the horse represents "the non-human psyche, the subhuman, animal side, the unconscious"; he relates it to the lower part of the body and the animal impulses that arise from there, saying it has dynamic power and "carries one away like a surge of instinct" (Jung, 1934b, par. 347).

3. Meltzer (1983, Chapter 11) clearly distinguishes the period of exploration of the dream from the period of analysis and "formulation" of the dream ("a transformation from visual to verbal language"); in that chapter, Meltzer describes his own method of dream-exploration and dream-analysis, should the reader want another example for comparison. Meltzer holds that the dream-exploration is the more important part of the process.

4. Jung's theory of archetypes has been challenged by those who do not believe that such patterns are *pre-existing* patterns that structure the psyche. Instead, theorists such as Jean Knox believe that these patterns "emerge" through typical interactions between the infant and their early care-givers (Knox, 2003), that is, archetypes are seen as "emergent" properties rather than pre-existing. An archetypal pattern such as that of the infant feeling terrified and killed off by the mother would *emerge* from the infant's experience of repeatedly feeling rejected by their mother and this rejection remaining unrepaired between them, so that the infant's powerful, generalized experience is of having been killed off by its mother.

CHAPTER SEVEN

Exploring some of the basics . . .
and not so basics

Associations

I t is one of the commonest errors, among both beginners and experienced therapists, to omit to ask the dreamer for their associations
to the dream and to think they know the meaning of certain dream
images, or even the whole dream, in advance. The therapist might be
correct in their understanding; however, they will invariably miss
vital elements of the dream. Frequently, however, the therapist is
substantially wrong, as dreamers will often have very particular associations that cannot be predicted. In addition, it makes for a much
richer experience, and one the dreamer is much more involved in, if
the dreamer gives their associations.

Ogden (1996) points out that while it is the client who dreams the
dream, yet the dream reflects the therapeutic work of both the client
and the therapist and is, therefore, in a significant way, a joint venture
(he describes this in terms of what he calls "the intersubjective analytic
third"). Ogden suggests that the therapist's own associations to the
dream, therefore, are also valid and important.

Ogden is writing from within the Freudian/psychoanalytic tradition, and some of what he is discussing as the therapist's associations

would be considered in the Jungian tradition as the therapist's amplifications relating to the archetypal level of the dream: for example,
amplification of the black horse image in the dream discussed above,
or Freud's association to/interpretation of the woman diving into the
lake. In the example Ogden gives, however, he describes his own
extensive personal associations, much as a client would normally give
(although he kept these mostly to himself); these were largely related
to the state of the therapeutic relationship.

Ogden might be criticized, as outlined earlier, for giving associations which lead away from the dream and simply reflect existing
resistances against the dream, rather than centring on and informing
the dream itself. I do occasionally offer my personal associations to a
client's dream, but do so tentatively, flagging up the fact that this is
my personal association. Furthermore, I will only give a very limited
number of associations, rather than a whole stream of them, as Ogden
describes in his example (Ogden, 1996, pp. 893 ff.).

For example, I recently suggested, after a client had given his associations to a dream, that the "three women dressed in black" that
appeared in the dream reminded me of the three witches in Shakespeare's *Macbeth*. The client said that, in fact, he had seen the play
himself only a few weeks before, something he had not mentioned to
me. The fact that he had not made the association to the witches was
striking, and we reflected more deeply on whether the play had
particular significance for the dreamer and in relation to the dream.
On other occasions, my personal associations have not struck a chord
with the dreamer.

A less contentious example is when the therapist simply reminds
the dreamer of possible associations; for example, whether the "girl in
the pink dress" in the dream might be related to the photograph of the
dreamer as a child that she once described, or whether the girl in the
pink dress relates to another dream in which there was a girl in a pink
dress.

Other considerations

It might take some time for the dreamer to give their associations; this
serves as good thinking time—reverie—for the therapist (and the
dreamer), where ideas about the dream can begin to take shape. Some

dreamers spontaneously give certain associations as they go along; for example, "this reminds me of the time when my father actually did have a car accident and I was in the back seat and bruised my leg, etc." This can be helpful, of course, in taking you deeper into the sense, feeling, and associative network of the dream, but I particularly note if I begin to lose track of what happened in reality and what happened in the dream, since that tends to indicate a similar mix up between dream and reality in the dreamer.

I do occasionally interrupt the dreamer to ask for associations before they have finished telling the dream, particularly if it is a long dream that is triggering no connections in me and particularly if the dream introduces an individual who appears to have a key role in the dream. For example, "In the dream I met Alison Jones, who I went to school with, and together we were climbing a steep hill, etc." I might interrupt the dreamer to ask what kind of person Alison Jones was/is. If I am told that Alison Jones was a timid girl who was sometimes bullied, I will listen to the dream thinking about whether, for example, the dream may be telling us something about a timid and sometimes bullied part of the dreamer.

The feeling in the dream

It can be particularly helpful to note what the dreamer's feeling is in a dream, or to ask about it if they have not volunteered it. This can serve to identify what is central to the dream. For example, in the dream discussed above, the feelings of pain and fear confirmed the focus on relationship. At other times, the feeling in the dream may be dissonant with the scenario of the dream: for example, "I won the lottery but I felt nothing", or "I was told I was dying but felt pleased". The unusual feeling will be signalling something very important that would need to be explored in relation to the dreamer's situation.

The feeling in a dream is particularly important, as one of the primary functions of dreaming is to work on, and work through, the emotional significance of the events that have occurred to which the dream refers. A dream of a "terrifying interview" might link to a "terrifying" time when the dreamer's father shouted at the dreamer for getting bad grades at school; it is not simply a matter of identifying "what" the dream is about, here, the traumatizing time with father, the dreaming of the dream is itself working on, and through, the terror, the trauma.

By reliving the traumatic affect, perhaps transposed to a different situation (from father shouting to the interview), the psyche is thought to be slowly detoxifying the traumatic feeling around that situation and integrating the memory in a manageable way; Jung would describe this as working through the powerful, distorting "complex" which has build up around the event. Chapter Eleven discusses both the emotional/affective nature of the work of dreams and its function in relation to memory; Chapter Twelve discusses repetitive traumatic dreams.

Domhoff reports on Kramer's study that Vietnam War veterans who had been able to work through the trauma of their experiences to some extent (working through their post traumatic stress disorder (PTSD)), and who had, thus, experienced a lessening of their repeated traumatic dreams of war, found that dreams relating to their war experience would recur when they began to experience current non-military life experience as conflictual. The conflict is being transposed to familiar (traumatic) territory (Kramer, Schoen, & Kinney, 1987, in Domhoff, 2001, p. 28).

The dreamer's sense of the dream

I will also usually ask if the dreamer has a sense of what the dream might refer to. I might put this in the form of "Is there anything that is going on at the moment that seems like this?" As discussed in the previous chapter, the dream is almost always trying to work on something that is currently preoccupying the dreamer, either consciously or unconsciously. A dream, for example, of a frantic dash not to miss a train might elicit few associations about trains, but may key in with the dreamer's sense that time is passing and they might miss the opportunity to have children; the dream is alerting the dreamer about just how "frantic" they are feeling about this, when they had felt consciously untroubled about it.

Troubleshooting: difficulties understanding a dream

It sometimes happens that the therapist and the dreamer can make no sense of the dream, despite the above processes. I think it is important, when the dream has been stayed with, struggled with, and sufficiently turned over, for the therapist to say as much. The feeling of satisfaction and "rightness" that comes when a dream interpretation does strike the right chord is so characteristic, and almost sacred, that it is important not to force the issue; as Jung says, "only what is really oneself has the power to heal" (Jung, 1928, par. 258). Sometimes, standing back and admitting that you "don't know" is just what is needed to liberate something in either the dreamer or therapist, and the clue might then "magically" appear—or it might not. As Hillman says, "the golden rule in touching any dream is keeping it alive. Dreamwork is conservation" (Hillman, 1979, p. 116).

Mantelpiece dreams

Hugh Gee (personal communication, 1993) calls dreams whose meaning is not clear at the time "mantelpiece dreams", as the dream can be put on the mantelpiece and returned to at a later time (Hugh puts other material that is unclear on his mantelpiece, too, not only dreams). There are some dreams, particularly powerful or uncanny dreams, that one returns to again and again, discovering a bit more of the meaning each time, or seeing the dream from a slightly different angle each time, thus gaining a broader view of its powerful influence. These he also considers mantelpiece dreams (see also the chapter on initial dreams).

When the interpretation is "not quite right"

Sometimes, an interpretation of a dream does not feel right to either the dreamer or the therapist, or both. Again, in the spirit of the joint work that is so necessary for dreams, it is important to say so. This leaves the dream open to be worked on further. I can sometimes hear from the tone of the dreamer's responses that an interpretation I have made has not struck a chord and, again, I will say as much. When the dreamer says that an interpretation does not feel right, this will often indicate that the dreamer has a sense of where the meaning does lie and careful questioning can then open up a new avenue for exploration.

No associations

Another common scenario is when no significant associations can be elicited for a particular image. This is particularly the case when the dream image is of a commonplace object. For example, a figure was wearing a blue shirt in the dream and the dreamer can think of no associations to a blue shirt. It can help to focus the dreamer back on the dream image itself (rather than trying to work out "what it means") by asking them to describe a blue shirt as if to someone who had never seen one, someone from another planet for example. The dreamer might then reply, "a shirt is a piece of clothing that you put on your upper body and that you wear every day", and "blue is a colour that I don't particularly like". Perhaps there is something the dreamer puts on every day, something to cover their "upper body", which they do not particularly like, such as some pretence or way of being at work, for instance.

It is important to say, however, that there are quite frequently images or aspects of images in dreams that do not get included in an interpretation; for example, with the dreamer in the horse dream, we did not particularly explore the image of the young woman's neck being broken (although I have offered an interpretation of that above). This may well be a loss; it may well be something that the dreamer and/or therapist may return to later, or it may be that the essence of the dream has been understood and there are more important things to discuss in this particular therapy at this particular time than this detail. Dreams are important, but must not be allowed to eclipse the main theme of any therapy—the dreamer's life!

Do we need to interpret dreams at all?

This raises the interesting question of whether we really need to interpret dreams at all, particularly if the process of dreaming is working on and working through the difficult-feeling material while we are asleep. As I describe further in Chapter Twelve, we have many dreams each night—as it is not possible to interpret *all* dreams, do we really need to interpret any?

In relation to this, the Kris Study Group conducted a study of dreams in analytic work and concluded that it was possible to identify the main themes that emerge through dreaming in the ordinary analytic material and free associations (Waldhorn, 1967, quoted in Blechner, 2001, p. 20). This conclusion appears to contradict Jung's assertion that dreams are fitted as nothing else to tell us what is really going on in the psyche, although Blechner suggests that the Kris Study Group's result follows precisely from the psychoanalytic practice of simply following the free associations away from the dream, a practice that Jung had criticized (Blechner, 2001, p. 21); in other words, they were treating the dream as a "just another association", rather than investigating it more thoroughly.

Although making the traumatic feeling-complex less powerful is an important aspect of dreaming, it is frequently necessary to become conscious of, and think about, a particular event in order to properly understand it and contain it. This is one of the fundamental tenets of psychoanalysis, which has been backed up by recent understandings in neuroscience. For example, we are able to come to "live with" certain traumatic events in our childhood by knowing about them, thinking about them, understanding why they happened, and what effect they had on our lives as well as those around us. The alternative is to be driven to act and enact things endlessly, for example, keeping people at arm's length because we fear a repeat of the intrusion we experienced in childhood. In the jargon, ego development occurs through the development of second order representations (conscious thoughts), which "contain" the more primitive affects (see Fonagy, Gergely, Jurist, & Target, 2002).

One might speculate that on waking (or on being woken by the dream), we particularly remember those dreams where the feeling content is powerful and requires that thinking work is done to properly deal with, detoxify, and contain it. Ogden (2004) describes nightmares as "interrupted dreams".

In regard to the Kris Study Group's assertion that dreams do not carry a special significance, since the material is available in the therapy anyway, it has certainly been my experience that when a therapy is working well, the dreams the client brings reflect what we are working on, although frequently they also present a useful additional commentary and perspective on it, deepening our understanding and making many more connections and links.

Frequently, however, it is a dream that presages and introduces a new theme when, perhaps, we have become stuck on something. While one could argue that those new developments or insights might have emerged anyway, this seems like a curious argument, as dreaming is an intrinsic part of the psyche; that the new material emerges through a dream is simply "the way it is".

There is one other unique contribution of dreams for me: they vitally "locate" something within the dreamer. One can say *there* is the sexually aggressive part of yourself, or the vulnerable, frightened part of yourself, or the heroic, capable, achieving part of yourself; in other words, "There it is, you have dreamt it". Of course, the dreamer could just say, "Oh, but that's just a dream!" However, I suggest that they would be denying something vital in themselves if they do so. By symbolizing these parts of the self so well, the dream informs us richly about these parts of ourselves; to repeat the quote from Jung, "a symbol is the best possible formulation of a relatively unknown psychic content" (Jung, 1922, par. 116).

How dreams are used

This raises the important question of how the dreamer uses dreams. Some people have a rich dream life and record all their dreams. If they bring all those dreams to once-weekly therapy, then the whole session could very well be taken up with exploring and interpreting dreams. Working on dreams can be a very satisfying and illuminating experience for both dreamer and therapist; however, even if transference level interpretations are brought in, for example "the man you hit over the head with a book in your dream was perhaps me and perhaps the book was the book you record your dreams in!", this can be treated by the dreamer as merely "something of interest" that their "unconscious" is getting up to. The dreamer does not really relate to what is being dreamt about, or to the therapist.

Dreams used defensively in this way can deaden the therapy and be something of an excursion from the real work of the therapy. The therapist is treated as a dream-interpreting functionary, safely under the dreamer's control, rather than a separate individual with their own thoughts, feelings, and responses, which can be a much more frightening prospect than even the worst nightmare! Kenneth Lambert gives examples of the way dreams may be given compliantly, or used to flood, deaden, belittle or induce helplessness in the therapist (1981, pp. 174–176). As Jung also says, one might easily be led to suppose that the dream is a kind of psychopomp which, because of its superior knowledge, infallibly guides life in the right direction. However much people underestimate the psychological significance of dreams, there is an equally great danger that anyone who is constantly preoccupied with dream-analysis will over-estimate the significance of the unconscious for real life. [Jung, 1948[1916], par. 494]

There needs to be a balance of focus

Follow-up dream

Jung described several series of dreams dreamt by his patients (1944, 1964, pp. 58 ff., 1984[1938]), as does Peters (1990) (see also Chapter Twelve of this book on series of dreams). I would like to describe just one further dream, linked to the horse dream described above.

Following that dream, the therapy naturally focused on the client's way of relating for several weeks and, in one session, he described to me how a female colleague at work had let slip that she had been talking about him to another colleague. He went on to say, in a characteristic manner, that he suspected it was something critical about him, as why else would they talk about him? I commented that I thought he was undervaluing himself, and I thought that as an eligible, single man he might be a ready topic of conversation at work among the women and that the conversation might equally be favourable about him. At the next session he reported the following dream:

> There is a horse race and one of the entries in the race was a horse that looks like a camel. A rider in the race says it all depends on his power, so I don't back him. I stand to watch the race on the course but as the horses come towards me/us, I have to get off the course to one side. I don't see it, but the camel-horse won the race.

I asked him if he had any associations to the camel-horse and he remembered the dream about the horse a few weeks before, but he said he could not think what the camel part might be. He described it as half camel and half horse, with long legs and a hump. He said he did not have any other thoughts about the dream and that it just seemed peculiar to him.

I reminded him that we had understood the horse in the previous dream to be related to his bodily desires and sexual needs, and I suggested that the camel is a creature that can travel a long way in the desert, having to provide its own sustenance. I wondered whether the camel-horse might therefore represent the part of him that has had to live alone, without the physical sustenance of a sexual relationship for a long time, as if he had been in the desert. The fact that the dreamer has to avoid the camel-horse in the dream may be another reference to his continuing fear of being overrun by sexual and needy feelings that are pressing to be recognized.

I also reminded him of my comment about him possibly being a source of positive discussion for the women in his workplace, and I wondered whether, although he may be sceptical about himself, others may have faith in him, just like the rider in the race who says it depends on the horse's power (his potency was an element in our discussion of the last dream). I pointed out that, in fact, the camel-horse had won the race, even though that seemed unlikely to him. He laughed at this interpretation and said it was like saying you have to have a bet on yourself—the interpretation seemed to have struck a chord.

CHAPTER EIGHT

Dream architecture: signs and symbols

Sometimes a cigar is just a cigar

possible construed use ·⎦

One of the hardest things for people new to interpreting dreams is to begin to make sense of the wealth of dream images and to orientate themselves within the dream. In my experience, and that of many others, there are certain dream images which commonly symbolize certain kinds of thing (they are arche-typal). I offer these as starting points for understanding the dream image, although an individual's personal associations to the image will usually have more significance and should be considered to take priority, even if the general, archetypal meanings might also apply.

Symbols and signs

To explore this caveat a bit further, one must be wary of immediately equating a dream image with a particular meaning, for example, horse equals body. Jung was critical of Freud in this respect. He thought that Freud interpreted symbols, which Jung thought had many layers of meaning, as signs that point to just one thing. For example, he accused Freud of interpreting anything pointed: a church steeple, a cigar, a pencil, a sword, a walking stick, etc., as a penis; and any container:

a handbag, a box, a coffin, a purse, a *cul-de-sac*, etc., as a vagina. As Jung put it, "You can say that a church spire is a phallic symbol but when you dream of a penis, what is that?" (Jung, 1957, p. 305, quoted in Colman, 2005, p. 641).

This kind of interpretation, equating sword and penis, would be in line with Freud's belief that the psyche is structured and dominated primarily by sexual and bodily impulses, so that dreams of a stick or a sword would represent these primary sexual features. Colman has pointed out that since the development of object relations theory, where the relationship itself is understood to be what is most valued, rather than just the sexual instinct, psychoanalysis has "come to regard sexuality and the body in metaphorical and symbolic terms" (Colman, 2005, p. 642).

In regard to dreams, this means that, by understanding the dream images as symbolic, they can be seen to refer to many more things than simply a satisfaction of the instinctual drive. So, while a sword might sometimes symbolize a penis, and a purse might sometimes symbolize a vagina, it is important to keep an open mind about this and recognize that it might symbolize something else as well, or something different on this occasion and in this particular context. For example, a handbag might symbolize where you keep important, valuable things; these things are not necessarily sexual in nature, but they might also be.

With these caveats, I would like to discuss certain dream images that have regularly been found to symbolize certain things. In saying this, I am saying exactly that these are archetypal. Jung explored the archetypal dimension of many images in an inimitable way, calling on myths and knowledge from all the great civilizations; see, for example, Volume 5 of his *Collected Works, Symbols of Transformation.*

I will be discussing just a few symbols and will call on those characteristics that can be intuitively understood to apply. Exploring the myths in the way that Jung did adds an extra layer of meaning and associations; for example, see his exploration of the symbol of the foot in the crab dream described in Chapter Five. I would warn that there is a chance that the extra layer of associations might, on occasion, lead one away from the core of the dream in a way not dissimilar to Jung's criticism of Freud. For instance, in his exploration of the myth of Isis and Set, there is quite a lot of extraneous material that is introduced relating to Isis being dismembered and eaten by fishes that might or might not be strictly relevant.

The house/flat

> I was in my flat but it was different from the way it actually is. I discovered a whole new set of rooms that were light and airy; there was a desk, pens, and paper, and lots of drawing materials. I felt excited and full of energy; I started dancing.

The state of the house tells us a great deal about the state of the person and their psyche at that time—the house/flat is "where the person lives". This dream heralded the dreamer rediscovering her creative abilities (the desk, pens, and paper) and vivacity (the airy rooms and the dancing), which had been effectively stifled and lost for some time.

Following on from Jung's dream of the house, the different elements and rooms of the house are important. The top floor or attic often symbolizes the head and "thinking", the kitchen where there is food and nourishment, the bedroom where there is intimacy and sex, and so on (although, again, the individual's particular associations to the bedroom, kitchen, or attic are important).

> There was a fire on the ground floor, which I ignored at first, but after a while the smoke started coming up the stairs and I went up to the attic and climbed out of the window in the roof. I walked away over the rooftops.

The dreamer associated the fire to anger, which we linked to anger that she was experiencing towards her boyfriend. Exploring the dream, we recognized that the dreamer had been ignoring this anger and dealing with it by rationalizing ("I expect the feelings will just go away soon") and daydreaming (thinking about her and her boy friend's forthcoming holiday). In this way, she had been escaping from the conflict (getting out of herself/the house) through daydreaming (going across the rooftops); this ignored the danger from the fire/anger or, more particularly, what it was in their relationship that was initiating the anger, which she was not taking into account . . . at her peril.

The state of the house in the dream is also very important:

there was a hole in the roof

there was one wall missing and everyone was looking in

the house was built precariously on a cliff edge

the house was derelict and had no furniture inside

These images may variously be trying to describe a state where the individual feels:

- insecure, narcissistically vulnerable, and "exposed to the elements" (the hole in the roof);
- exposed to the view of others with their essential security compromised (a wall missing);
- not in a stable and viable place psychologically (on a cliff edge);
- experiencing little care or comfort (the house is derelict with no furniture).

Dreams of staying in a hotel often symbolize more transitory states of mind, in other words, states you stay in for a short time rather than "live in", states you pass through rather than "who you are".

Cars, bicycles, and motorbikes

These personal means of transport are the means by which we "get around in the world". I have frequently found that, unless there is some contra-indication, they symbolize the dreamer's personality and, therefore, the way they relate to others; Jung would call this their persona.

> I was driving in a car that was old and decrepit
>
> I couldn't find anywhere to park
>
> I had parked somewhere but I couldn't find my car
>
> I crashed into the side of a posh, executive car
>
> I was not in control of the car and was driving dangerously in the middle of the road
>
> I was cycling through London and I kept getting lost

These are dream fragments which, on discussion with the dreamer, we felt were describing the dreamer's sense that:

- they were behaving in outmoded ways and felt ashamed of themselves (the old and decrepit car);
- they could not find a way of being comfortable with others and felt they did not fit in (nowhere to park);

- they had lost a sense of "who they were" and how to relate (could not find their car);
- they were feeling envious and angry with authority figures, with whom they were having arguments (crashing into a posh, executive car);
- they felt out of control and in danger of having conflict with others in a way that felt as if it could be fatal (not in control, driving in the middle of the road);
- they did not know how to navigate through life, feeling lost (getting lost in London). I have frequently found that London, as the capital city of England, is used to symbolize the central, core self by dreamers living in England.

Trains, planes, and buses

One client used to frequently dream of trains and going on train journeys; these were frequently pleasant enough journeys, but perhaps there was some difficultly getting the right train, or changing trains at the right point, or getting all her baggage on to the train. We often thought of these dreams in terms of her personal journey and the journey of the therapy: Could she get to where she wanted to go? Was she going the right way or in the right therapy? What was happening to her "baggage" (the issues she was bringing with her)?

It was notable that she was a laid-back person who used to "go with the flow". On a train, one is a passenger, and the train travels in a fixed direction. One can choose to get on and off the train, but one does not have close control over where it goes. Similarly, my client used to be very attuned to how others affected her and, as a consequence, used to be wary of getting into an intimate relationship because of the bad effect the other person might have on her. She felt able to "be herself" best when she was living alone.

It was striking that not long after she began dreaming of going on journeys in her car, she unexpectedly started a new, intimate relationship. I suggest that her dreams of driving her car indicated that she was able to take more control over her own direction rather than putting herself so much in the hands of others; she was prepared to struggle for herself more, rather than just "change trains" if things were not going in the right direction.

Plane journeys and flying have a number of different characteristics that the dream may be trying to symbolize: a question of trust and being in the pilot's hands; being "up in the air", not grounded, and potentially in danger of coming down to earth with a bang; and a certain mastery and exuberance (that may not last forever—"what goes up must come down"), to name just three elements.[1]

> I was on a plane. I had a terrible sense that we were going to crash.

In this instance, the individual felt that her mood, which was often changeable, was about to come crashing down. The dream helped her to recognize that there was something unrealistic about her "high" state of mind.

> I was flying in a really small plane trying to get to X. We crashed, but I got up and walked away unhurt. I carried on my journey.

This person "didn't have her feet on the ground" and lived somewhat in her head, keeping her gut reactions at arm's length. As we explored the dream, it seemed that part of her was recognizing that coming down to earth was not so bad, it was survivable and all part of her journey.

Freud thought that dreams of flying (under one's own power) or falling, accompanied by either pleasurable feelings or feelings of anxiety, probably relate to childhood experiences of play and, in particular, of being swung playfully by adults. He suggests that such dreams frequently relate to early sexual experience that might have accompanied them (Freud, 1900a, pp. 270 ff.). I have found that dreams of flying often relate to exuberant feeling states that rely predominantly on the individual's emotions and moods and are not sustainable states of mind. Similarly dreams of falling reflect insecure feeling states where, again, there is no sense of a substantial, stable structure (in dream terms, an aeroplane or hang-glider) to sustain the individual—the person feels they are unheld and "falling" or they are exhilarated at being able to "stay up".

"closed off" symbolism

Journeys

I have mentioned the journeying on trains and planes, and journeys of some kind or another are very frequent elements in dreams; one is often trying to get somewhere, or travelling somewhere. It is not too hard to interpret what it might mean if the dreamer is "struggling uphill" or "slipping backwards toward a precipice" or "driving on a flooded field", but it is important to also consider these journeys on the transference level as referring to the dreamer's experience of the therapy, as well as their journey and development in life. A client just coming to the end of the counselling required for his training brought the following dream in his penultimate session:

> I was with a band of Native American Indians walking through forests and hills with some of our people and animals—a bit like a hunting party—we were finally returning to our homelands, having been away for a time.

This was a poignant dream under the circumstances. His associations were that the Native American Indians were a free people, who lived close to nature and rejected the ways of modern life. If we ask, "what is going on in your current life that might be like this?", the ending of the counselling was clearly significant. The question seemed to be, was the homecoming brought about through the counselling or was the home-coming only coming about because the counselling was ending?

On reflection, it seemed that this dream was offering the client and counsellor an understanding of the limitations of the counselling. The dreamer admitted that he had not felt fully able to be himself in the counselling (the Native American Indians living close to nature) and he had felt the counsellor had wanted him to be a certain way and had put implicit pressure on him to be that way (the ways of modern life).

The ending of a therapy is an opportunity to look frankly at what has been achieved in the therapy and what has not (there are always going to be some issues left unresolved). This dream allowed the counsellor and client to reflect on the parts of himself that the client had not been able to bring to the counselling; he went on to further therapy later. The dream also gave the counsellor the opportunity to consider the kinds of subtle pressure she was putting on her clients to "get better", or to be a certain way. This is an example of the transference level of dreams serving as supervision for the therapist (see Chapter Five for further discussion of this subject).

The elements

The elements—earth, air, fire, and water—are frequently featured in dreams. These can be explored and amplified with reference to the four basic elements described by the Hindu, Buddhist, Babylonian, Japanese, Greek, and Chinese traditions;[2] Jung was also interested in exploring the alchemical and astrological systems related to the elements. Alchemy was originally a system for trying to understand matter itself. The elements, earth, air, fire, and water, when they appear in dreams are frequently used to represent groundedness/hard reality (earth), thinking/phantasy (air), passion (fire), and emotion (water).

Water

The presence of water in different forms and states will usually, unless there is something contra-indicating, symbolize emotion:

> the sea was rough and stormy, we were being tossed around in a small boat
>
> a tidal wave was coming up the road
>
> the waves were breaking gently against the shore
>
> I was being swept along by a broad, fast-flowing river
>
> I was in swimming pool but I couldn't see the bottom, things were lurking underneath

I probably do not need to suggest what kind of feeling states these are symbolizing; it is natural for us to see and even to describe our feelings in such ways: "I feel as if I've been hit by a tidal wave", "my feelings have been turbulent", and so on. I do not think that it is just because I live on the South Coast of England that many people bring dreams about the sea and the shore, which I understand to symbolize the current state of the relationship between their "watery", fluid feelings and their "solid" thinking: is the sea about to inundate the land? Are the waves crashing over houses on the shoreline? Or are the waves calmly breaking on the shore, accompanied by a sense of equilibrium?

Of course, where the observer is in the dream will be significant: are they swimming in the ocean with no sign of land? Up against the shore with the tide coming in and no way to scramble up the rocks? Standing on the cliffs watching a massive wave advancing? Or trying to cross a river and getting bitten by a crab? If we imagine how we might feel in these situations, we can perhaps get a sense of the

"threat" of the advancing feelings: from terror of inundation to trepi-
dation at being bitten (see Jung's interpretation of the crab in the river
dream in Chapter Five).

Land

The land is, of course, likely to be equally telling: is the dreamer climbing a dangerous rocky mountain? Sliding down a slippery bank
towards an abyss? Climbing a never-ending hill? Stuck and exposed
on a snowy mountain, unable to proceed? Trekking across a dry
desert? All these describe various difficulties and challenges with the
"solid" land: negotiating dangerous "rocky" hazards; getting nowhere
on a never-ending ascent; stuck and exposed with a seemingly insu-
perable problem; in a dry place without the basic requirements for
existence (water / emotion / relationship).

Fire

Fire, typically, symbolizes some kind of passion: a particular emotion
that might consume and inflame the individual, often / usually caus-
ing damage; look, for example, at the fire in the house dream I
discussed earlier. Fire, therefore, frequently symbolizes the individual's state of mind where they are being consumed with envy, jealousy, greed, or hatred (fire "consumes" what it burns), or inflamed
with rage, lust, pain, or outrage.

   To look at fire in a dream on the objective level for a moment, Jung
describes a dream where a patient dreamt that his former doctor died
in a great fire. Within three weeks the doctor did, in fact, die of a
deadly gangrenous fever (Jung, 1964, p. 66); the patient had intuited
something important about the doctor. Jung reports that Artemidorus
of Daldis, in the second century AD, reported a similar dream where a
man dreamt that his father died in a house fire and himself died a few
weeks later of a high fever.

Air

"Air" is archetypally related to thinking and phantasy and is
frequently featured in dreams of being at a great height, flying (see
above), or being at the top of the house or a skyscraper.

I was at the theatre in the upper circle. I looked over the edge of the balcony and knocked something off which fell and hurt an Indian man in the audience below. He was carried out of the theatre on a stretcher.

This dream was brought near the beginning of therapy and the dreamer recognized that she was not very grounded. Over time, we explored how she lived with her head in the clouds, somewhat out of touch with her feelings, and that, in particular, in relationships she could cut off from others, leaving them to experience the hurt as she withdrew (the Indian man was hurt by what had fallen from the balcony). Her association to this figure was that she particularly loved India, although she recognized the hardship there, and had great respect for the Indian people and their rich culture. We understood that she wanted and needed to get in touch with the more "Indian" part of herself that could experience hardship and that getting in touch with this part might bring her "cultural richness". Her way of going about things previously had been rather "special" and she could in some ways look down on people (she was in the upper circle of the theatre).

To some, these links might be obvious, but it is exactly building up experience with such dream images that makes orientating yourself within the dream that much easier. If you have to start from scratch with each dream, it can be daunting and more than a little hard going; it is good to have some basic hypotheses to start from and to test out, but do not take any of these thoughts as hard and fast rules; that would be taking symbols to be signs.

Notes

1.   Edinger (1972, p. 27) linked flying dreams with the myth of Icarus, refer-encing the archetypal level of the dream; dreams of being bitten by a snake he related to the Garden of Eden, where a new state of conscious-ness comes through the snake's intervention (ibid., p. 22).

2.   The theory of the elements was put forward by Empedocles of Acragas [495–435 bc] and taken up and developed by Aristotle. The Chinese tradi-tion has five elements: fire, earth, and water, but with metal and wood instead of air.

CHAPTER NINE

The position of the "I": death, violence, marriage, sex, gender, toilets, time, and location

In this chapter, I look at some of the other important information that can be gleaned from a dream, in particular:

- the position of the "I" in the dream: is the dreamer the subject of the dream (is the dream happening to them) or is the dreamer looking on, watching the main action happen to someone else? Are they in a film or a play, or even asleep or drugged?;
- some possible symbolic meanings of death, violence, marriage, sex, gender, and bodily functioning;
- the time setting of the dream: the mix of past, present and future;
- the location: what can be told from the "background" of the dream.

The position of the "I" in the dream

The relation of the dreamer—the "I"—to the other figures and the action of the dream tells us a great deal about how much the dreamer is identified with (and perhaps also, therefore, conscious of) the issues that are being dreamt about; in other words, how much they are a part of how the dreamer sees themselves and, thus, integrated into their ego, or, instead, not yet integrated and part of the dreamer's shadow.[1]

Compare the following dreams:

> I was being chased by a crocodile and was running and running, trying to get away. I felt frantic and terrified.

And

> I was in a fight and the man pulled out a knife and stabbed me. To my surprise I wasn't killed and I got away.

Here, the dreamers are struggling with what feels like a central threat to their existence, whether in the form of some voracious, needy/greedy "animal" part or an aggressive, murderous part (of themselves or someone else). In contrast:

> I was watching a man being beaten up; there was a gang of youths kicking him. He looked very afraid and stopped moving, I thought he was probably dead.

Here, the dreamer is not feeling the same sense of threat and is not as centrally involved; the main action of the dream is happening to someone else, which might possibly symbolize part of the dreamer that they are not in touch with (it is one of the basic tenets of psychoanalysis that we have to *discover* what we think and feel, and who we are). These might be vulnerable or aggressive qualities that we do not necessarily see as parts of ourselves but see instead as primarily in other people, in other words, they are projected.[2]

While this young man had been brought up in a large family, he had not felt overtly threatened or "beaten up" himself. Instead, he had become depressed and felt that he could not find his place in the world, becoming despairing of being able to find the right kind of work for himself. In interpreting the dream, we saw that an internal "gang" mentality had practically killed off his self (the man being beaten up), but that he was detached from this self and this had been part of the cause of his depression.

This gang mentality took the form of his own expectations that, as a man, he should be decisive, know what he wanted to do, and be successful. These were expectations that he felt both his family and society espoused and which he had taken in largely unquestioned. Part of our work, following on from the dream, was to think about what he really valued and wanted for himself; as it turned out, this *cultural* had little to do with being decisive and successful in the traditional *Kor* sense.   *& West*

Jung called the deepest part of the unconscious the collective unconscious, and was clear that one element of the process of individuation is to be able to distinguish one's own views from the views of the collective. Quite often, gangs or groups in dreams represent the undeveloped "collective" parts of the dreamer, as in this case.[3] In order to properly free himself from these collective values, the dreamer had to connect with his own "gang of youths" and to be prepared to kick and fight for what he believed in.

An example of movement of the "I"

I watched a little furry animal running around desperately, then I was that animal, but I had wings. I flew off.

Animals quite frequently symbolize particular parts of the dreamer, frequently the less developed, shadow parts, for example, lion, wolf, hyena, squirrel, worm, etc. In this dream, the "I" is shifting from outside looking on to "becoming" the main figure (the little furry animal). This would indicate a shift in the dreamer's state from looking on at the "furry animal's" distress to identifying more closely with that animal and "flying off". The dreamer said she thought the fluffy animal was "small, defenceless, and frightened". We could see that she sometimes felt herself to be like that, and we were able to explore the way that she "took flight" when she felt threatened, and, in particular, if and when she felt threatened in the therapy.

Hillman (1979, 1983) writes a good deal about animals in dreams, although he is, in general, against the "interpretative method of dream analysis": Hillman says that we should "stick with the image", as only this way can we keep the image alive. His concern is that in defining, for example, the image of a snake in a dream, and interpreting it, you lose the snake, and the client leaves the session with a concept about their "repressed sexuality" or "cold black passions". Hillman's essential point is that a dream image should not be reduced to an interpretation. I would argue that a dream tells us about a part of ourselves, and that knowing about and understanding it also helps us to include it as a living presence within us.

Hillman would differ from the method adopted in this book, however, in that he would emphasize imaginatively exploring the little furry animal/snake image in more detail: What was it like to be that animal? What kind of fur did it have? What was it like to have fur? Where was it running around? Why was it desperate? What did that feel like? This process, known as active imagination, is in the service of keeping the image alive and puts the dreamer more in touch with the felt experience of the dream.

Dissociation

Sometimes the distance of the dreamer from the action in the dream is specifically symbolized. This can signify that the dreamer is, in some way, living an unreal life through feeling detached from whatever the issue is, or being simply an onlooker unable to affect it:

> I was watching a film and there was a lot of action and danger but I was sitting there feeling bored.

> I was asleep and I couldn't wake up. I kept hearing a voice shouting "Wake up! Wake up! Wake up!" but I could do nothing about it.

Or the example from Chapter Six:

> . . . I move to go and help but don't as I'm too afraid to lose my life.

In the first of these three dreams, the dreamer is registering the boredom that followed from her cut-off state. In the second dream, there is a sense of urgency that is trying to wake the dreamer from his sleep/unconsciousness, although ultimately there is a sense of hopelessness, as the dreamer does not wake (in the dream). In the therapy, we explored what it was that he was not "waking up" to, something he could identify pretty readily when asked.

It is worth noting that in a film or play, the dialogue is often given; this may symbolize that a particular "script" is being enacted by the dreamer, which may relate to early relational patterns (attachment patterns/ways of being with others) laid down in the unconscious, as discussed in Chapters Four and Five.

Whitmont and Perera (1989, pp. 18–19) give a good example of the way the dream-ego is portrayed from the point of view of the unconscious "guiding" self (see Chapter Three): a man who consciously thought of himself as caring and helpful dreamt that,

> I am asked to rescue a hurt child. Instead of going to the scene of the pain, I send my handkerchief.

Whitmont and Perera report that, with some difficulty, as well as a sense of assent, the dreamer was able to recognize the dream as a true picture of his refusal to take real responsibility, replacing real caring (including of his own inner child) with token, genteel gesturing (sending the handkerchief). This is another good example of the compensatory aspect of a dream.

Death, violence, marriage, sex, and bodily functions

These very concrete activities are frequently used symbolically in dreams. In death, something is passing away—it is important to consider what it is that is dying off. The dream about the man being attacked by the gang so that he "stopped moving" and was "probably dead" is a good illustration of a part of the self that is dying.

Von Franz gives an example from her own experience where, after a day of feeling the nearness of death, she dreamt that a romantic young boy had died (1980, pp. 17–18; quoted in Hall, 1983, p. 24). She understood this as an idealistic male part of herself losing its influence (an "animus" figure—see below).

Dreams where the dreamer him/herself dies symbolize that a central way of being, with which the dreamer is primarily identified (is central to their ego), is "dying"; for example:

> I was told that I had cancer of the digestive system and was dying. I felt fiercely pleased that my mother would have to deal with that.

The dreamer said that his mother had, in fact, worried about everything (she had not been able to "digest" difficulties) and, as a result, he had often had to worry about her and look after her; in the dream he now had cancer of his own "digestive system".

The dream also told us about his own detached attitude towards himself (he was not worried that he was dying). This detachment probably developed due to his mother's self-preoccupation, so that, as she had not been properly available to him (to have wanted her to care for him would have been too painful in the long run), he had learnt to defend himself by cutting off from his feelings.

In the dream, he takes revenge on his mother and is "fiercely pleased" that she will have to deal with his death; he is pleased to be imposing uncomfortable feelings on her rather than protecting her from them. In this sense, the dream is a compensation for what had been his conscious attitude towards his mother; perhaps it is the part of himself that is concerned primarily for others that is dying off—it had proved cancerous and fatal to his true self.

Toilets and bodily functions

This dream about cancer of the digestive system takes us close to another theme that frequently occurs in dreams, that of defecation and urination. People frequently dream of trying to find a toilet, or getting there to find it occupied, or dirty, or in an exposed place; sometimes they are looking to urinate, sometimes to defecate. These natural functions often symbolize how we get rid of, or find difficulty in getting rid of, our psychological waste matter, either the more solid, long-lasting "shitty feelings" that we carry inside us, and which we may be ashamed of or which may "make a bad smell", or the more fluid, immediate hot-wet-angry urine feelings/waste. Obviously, the particular meaning will relate to the context of the dream, although, as always, be aware of particular personal associations; Jung reports one patient's dream where the urge to urinate related to marriage, as the dreamer had once wet himself, at the age of eleven, when he was attending a long marriage ceremony (Jung, 1909, pars 92–93).

Back to death

Another dream that treats death symbolically:

> I got a phone call from my cousin who said that my aunt [his mother] was alive and did I want to come round to see her? When I put the phone down I thought that can't be right as she is dead [she is in fact dead]. I was confused and wondered if my cousin had made it up. I was telling a psychiatrist I know about this and I became convinced that I was having hallucinations and had a brain tumour. I went to hospital where I was given an injection to get rid of the hallucinations. I felt odd and passed out. I didn't want to be in the hospital and ran away and hid with other people—drug addicts and drop-outs. Then it changed into me being with pirates on a pirate ship and the captain really liked me, he stood behind me and hugged me, I was the special cabin boy.

The dreamer told me that, in fact, she felt she had been her aunt's favourite, favoured over her own children, which had been particularly important to her as her own mother had not made her feel at all special, in fact, just the opposite—unloved and rejected. In the dream, she was put out that her aunt was back with her cousin but was also trying to work out how and whether she was alive again; it was something that was driving her to feel that she was mad/hallucinating.

Our exploration of the dream led us to look at whether she felt she was special to me now, in the transference, and how this was confusing/maddening to her—was her aunt (the specialness) alive or dead? This was her Oedipal struggle, to be able to accept that she did not have to be the special one to be all right and that I could have a relationship with my own family and other patients and that that could be bearable to her. This was difficult for her, as she felt that the cure—the injection/therapy that would stop her hallucinating her aunt/wanting to be special—made her feel odd and left her feeling like a drop-out or drug addict: in other words, rejected and not good or special. Her resolution was to try to get some of this specialness "by hook or by crook", like a pirate. She did this by trying to become special to me and to her boss at work (whom she associated to the captain of the pirate ship), but the dream was telling her that she was doing something piratical and forceful (taking what she wanted even if it was not hers, like a pirate).

Freud thought that one of the characteristics of the unconscious was the "absence of mutual contradiction"; sometimes a dreamer will see no contradiction in someone being alive and dead in a dream, unlike here. This apparent contradiction can be reconciled when we consider what it is that is being symbolized. Here, it was a question of whether the dreamer was special or not, and the appearance or disappearance of feeling special to someone. This was symbolized by the aunt being dead or alive.

This is an example which bears out Matte Blanco's analysis of the unconscious, as described in Chapter Four, where the unconscious recognizes the sameness—the symmetry—between the aunt and being special. It is this understanding that makes the dream comprehensible rather than contradictory. It is not so much a function of "the unconscious" as a function of the way symbols are formed, with different things being associated in some way: here, the aunt and being special. Being special to someone can be "dead" and then "alive", aunts cannot.

Violence

> I was in a fight with a man and was using a lot of martial arts moves, but he was good, too. I fought back hard and he didn't kill me.

Violence and fights can stand for different kinds of "engagement", whether it is an example of competitiveness, a struggle for power, or even a form of sexual encounter (particularly if the fight is with a knife, sword, or stave—traditional Freudian "phallic symbols"). It is worth remembering that we can feel as if we have been attacked/ struck/hit by a rejecting comment, and it is this gut level equation of attack = violence which is frequently portrayed in dreams. The dreamer and I explored this dream in terms of the sparring nature of our early sessions, where he was pleased to find that he could stand up to me and that he was not killed off by our encounters. (See Chapter Thirteen for a discussion of recurring traumatic dreams.)

Marriage, sex, and gender

Similarly, sex and marriage in dreams often symbolize some other kind of intercourse or linking up. Particularly important in Jungian theory is the contra-sexual aspect of the individual: the male aspect of a woman, known as the *animus,* and the female aspect of a man, known as the *anima.* These concepts have now been accepted into common culture, so that it is commonplace to hear talk of a man's feminine side, or a woman's masculine side. When Jung proposed these archetypal formulations in the 1920s, the gender roles in society were much more rigid and the concepts probably seemed more radical than they do to us today.

In fact, there has been a general "drift" in the use of these terms from the way Jung originally defined them (Jung, 1921), so that men and women are now referred to as having both an anima and an animus, in other words, both inner masculine and inner feminine qualities, rather than just one. In Jung's day, he took it that a man would be primarily identified with the masculine aspects of his personality (with the anima naturally being secondary and undeveloped), and, similarly, that a woman would naturally be identified with the feminine aspects of her personality (with the animus being the unconscious figure): in other words, the man only had an anima and the woman only an animus.

> I was at work and met a really attractive man, we flirted for a while then we had fantastic sex in my boss's office.

> I met a young woman, old enough to be my daughter, and we fell in love and got married.

These dreams were dreamt by a married woman and a married man, respectively. Such dreams are frequently reported with some difficulty and embarrassment as, taken on the concrete, objective level they seem to be about infidelity and some kind of incestuous relationship. Dreams of having sex with men are also sometimes reported by men whose primary sexual orientation is heterosexual and who are shocked by such dreams, and, similarly, homosexual dreams in heterosexual women are also quite common. It is important, of course, to explore whether there is some actual sexual attraction that may be being referred to in the dream, but in these cases that did not seem to be the primary focus at this time.

The first dream was dreamt by a woman who had been quite timid and retiring when I first met her, but, through the course of the therapy, had become increasingly assertive and successful. The key element in the dream was that the affair had occurred at work, and it seemed that the dreamer had connected with her attractive, assertive, masculine qualities (her animus) in a way that was energizing and exciting, symbolized by the "fantastic sex" in the dream. We speculated as to whether she felt able now to compete with her boss and potentially take over her role and her office. Having explored this, we also looked at whether she felt our "engagement" in the therapy, which was lively and challenging at times, represented "fantastic sex" and had contributed to her feeling more potent.

Similarly, the dreamer of the second dream had been staid and stereotypical in his old-fashioned views on masculinity, and was significantly cut off from his feelings. We understood the sex and the marriage to the young woman to represent his daring and almost forbidden connection to, and integration of, his young, vulnerable, feminine qualities. The shocking nature of both dreams (to the dreamers, if taken concretely) represents the shocking innovation to their personalities. Jung wrote a good deal concerning incest as a symbol, which expresses the need for new elements of the personality, held in the unconscious, to be taken notice of (e.g., Jung 1911–1912, pars 332, 450).

Julius Caesar famously dreamt of having intercourse with his mother the night before crossing the Rubicon to march, successfully, on Rome. His dream interpreters reasoned that Caesar's mother represented Rome, his mother country, and that the dream foretold that she would receive him. This is clearly an Oedipal dream, as Freud himself noted (Freud 1900a, p. 397n), and we can see that Caesar was about to overthrow the old, "father" order of rule in order to possess mother-Rome for himself.

Are we to take this Oedipal dream (as Jung might have) as symbolizing the need for the rigid old order to be overthrown to allow in the new (unconscious) forces of progress? Or should we heed the Oedipal warning and suggest that Caesar was blinded by ambition (just as Oedipus later blinded himself in the myth) and that in overthrowing the old order of rule, Caesar set up the line of Emperors which led directly to the fall of the Roman Empire? Both scenarios are inherent in the dream.

Location, time, and age

Dreams are almost always located somewhere (unless there is just a dream fragment) and these background facts often tell us a great deal about the dream itself.

I was on a hill and it was raining . . .

I was somewhere dark but I couldn't see where clearly . . .

I was in my parents' house . . .

I was in my house, but it was different to the way it actually is . . .

I don't know where I was . . .

All these locations, which hardly need suggested interpretations from me, help set the scene of the dream and point to the sense, feeling, and meaning of the dream. Imaginatively and empathically "feeling your way into" the dream gives a good sense of its meaning, for example, exposed in a rainy place, in the dark and uncertain, etc., etc.

Time frames, like locations, are frequently mixed up in dreams, which again reflects Freud's understanding of the unconscious as having the characteristics of timelessness and absence of mutual contradiction (or we can see simply as there being something similar in both scenarios (Chapter Four)). Consider these dream fragments:

I was back at school but it wasn't like it actually was, it was more like the building where I work.

In this dream, there is something going on at the dreamer's work that makes the dreamer feel as if they are at school. The dreamer's feeling association to school was that it was a "grim place where I was unhappy most of the time". It did not take us long to identify which aspects of his work felt similarly grim to him now.

I was a child in the house I lived in until I was seven years old and . . .

The age of the dreamer is also frequently altered from fact, so that we can feel that we are anything from a child to an old person—or even a foetus to a 1000-year-old man. The age of the figure in the dream reflects the state of mind that the dreamer is struggling with, whether it is the sensitive, frightened, dependent, happy child; the carefree, bolshie, rebellious, adventurous adolescent; the strict, concerned, fertile, mature adult; or the wise, experienced, frail, failing old man/woman and so on.

Common or typical dreams

Jung and Freud both wrote about common dreams of falling, flying, being persecuted by dangerous animals or hostile men, being insufficiently clothed in public places, being in a hurry or lost in a crowd, one's teeth falling out, fighting with useless weapons or being wholly defenceless, running hard and getting nowhere, growing infinitely large or small or being transformed from one to the other. Freud explored such dreams in a lot more detail (Freud, 1900a, pp. 339 ff), while Jung saw them as motifs that he thought should be considered in the context of the dream itself (Jung, 1964, pp. 38 ff).

Jung gives an example of a dream where the dreamer is riding on horseback across a wide field. The dreamer is in the lead and jumps a ditch full of water, while his companions fall into the ditch. Jung says that he has heard this dream from two different individuals and that it had a different meaning for each: one was a cautious, introverted young man, the other an old man who was taking risks with his health and acting against doctors' orders. Jung suggests that, for the young man, the dream was encouraging him to take the risk and that he would clear the obstacle, while, for the older man, the dream was warning him that he was taking too many risks with his health and that while he had "cleared the fence" on this occasion, he might not be so lucky in the future (Jung, 1964, p. 56).

It is clear that such motifs reflect the human condition; for example, we all sometimes feel cautious, frightened, defenceless, overpowered, over-exposed, or embarrassed; perhaps such dreams also depict our struggles with the mammalian defence systems of hyper-vigilance, fight, flight, freeze, and submission that are common to us all, as reflected in dreams of worry, wariness, fighting, fleeing, powerlessness, being unable to move, failure, and loss.[4]

Notes

1. Peters writes very interestingly on the subject of the dream ego in his book, *Living with Dreams* (1990).
2. Jung said that if you want to find out what is in your shadow (the unknown, denied, and repressed parts of yourself) think about what you do not like in others.

3. Rosenfeld (1971) writes of the inner Mafia-like gang that advocates regression and painlessness rather than real, "live" relationships.

4. The neuroscientist Jaak Panksepp holds that there is no evidence for biological defence systems dedicated to these behaviours *per se*, although he acknowledges that such behaviours do exist (Panksepp 1998, p. 203 & fn. 95). He suggests that such behaviours emerge from the RAGE and PANIC systems that he outlines, for which he presents good evidence (he also outlines SEEKING, CARE, LUST, and PLAY systems).

CHAPTER TEN

The initial dream

"Initial dreams which appear at the very outset of the treatment, often bring to light the essential aetiological factor in the most unmistakable way"

(Jung, 1934b, par. 296)

"Initial dreams are often amazingly lucid and clear-cut. But as the work of analysis progresses, the dreams tend to lose their clarity"

(*ibid.*, par. 313)

D reams that are dreamt near the beginning of a therapy often capture the essence of the issues which have brought the individual to therapy. A patient had the following dream soon after beginning:

I was sitting in a compartment of a railway carriage (one of the old-fashioned ones that seated only six people). All the seats were taken. My mother came into the carriage and I had to give up my seat for her. The next thing, I was hanging on the outside of the train as it was hurtling along. I was terrified.

This was a dream that we returned to on many occasions over the years, simply referring to it as "the railway carriage dream" after a while. We built up a rich understanding of its symbolism that told us a good deal about the dreamer's conflicts and difficulties. Over time, we explored the dream on the following levels and in the following ways.

The objective level

It was relatively easy for us to recognize the way that the dreamer had felt displaced by her mother's demands as a child (as in the dream she is displaced by her mother in the carriage), as the whole household had revolved around her mother and her moods. This pattern was still continuing in adulthood as, although my client ostensibly disliked her mother, she felt bound to her, talked about her in the therapy above everything else, and was preoccupied by her relationship with her in both practical and emotional ways.

The subjective level

If we treat all the elements of the dream as aspects of the dreamer, we can see that the mother figure in the dream could symbolize both her feelings about her mother and her own needy, demanding feelings. She is displaced and dominated both by her preoccupation with her mother and by her own needs, which carried her along like a passenger on the outside of a train. She herself could be like her mother to the extent that these needy aspects of herself dominated her personality; in this way, other parts of herself were less well developed and were displaced, in particular her sense of self-agency. She experienced herself as dangerously driven by her feelings (the train) and having to go where they took her, feeling very exposed and vulnerable (hanging on the outside).

The transference level

It was clear from early on in the therapy that the dreamer felt she would be expected to fit in with me and that she displaced herself and her feelings in order to do so. It was not that I expected or demanded this, of course, that was simply the pattern that my client was used to and, furthermore, it was the way she avoided conflict and sought closeness between us. When, over time, her suspended feelings mounted in intensity, they would return, taking her over, and it could equally well be me who then experienced what it was like to be "clinging dangerously to the outside of a train", as the therapy became dominated by the power of her feelings and her desperation about "what to do". At these times, it felt as if the therapy had a direction and a momentum of its own, of which neither of us was in control. It sometimes felt as if I was expected to fit in with the dreamer (giving up my seat in the carriage) and that she had become like her demanding mother, something that she was appalled to recognize. Similarly, she could feel taken over by the therapy itself as the feelings that emerged in therapy took her over and dominated her.

The archetypal level

We can see all three characteristics of archetypal functioning here: as a general/typical pattern, as related to early functioning, and as powerful and important. There is a part of all of us that is, perhaps, prepared to sacrifice our own position and viewpoint, and perhaps even our whole selves, in order to fit in with others at times, perhaps just for "a quiet life". There are consequences of this choice in terms of displacement and the compulsion that comes from our unmet needs and our unexpressed self, which this dream expresses so well. I see this as an emergent archetypal pattern that, if not balanced by other factors, can solidify into a hysterical personality organization (West, 2007, Chapter 9).

For my client, this archetypal pattern represented her predominant "way of being with others" (Stern, 1985), as her mother had been preoccupied with herself throughout my client's childhood and had been uninterested in responding to my client except in so far as she furthered her own desires (her mother had been intensely narcissistic). These early patterns of interaction had come to dominate and determine her later relationships and functioning. Even if we become conscious of behaving in these ways, we cannot simply change them by wishing to do things differently. These patterns have to be painstakingly worked through in the therapy in the hope that the most problematic aspect of any such patterns may be ameliorated. For my client, this meant coming to experience herself as independent and separate from me and developing her own sense of agency and direction (not being carried along by trains).

It goes without saying that this dream was powerful and important for the dreamer in that it captured the essence of her difficulties so well, although it was not numinous and larger than life in the sense described in Chapter Five. Kradin has written an interesting book which focuses particularly on initial dreams, which he calls "herald dreams" (Kradin, 2006).

Do you ask for dreams?

Dreams are so important that sometimes therapists will ask clients at their first meeting whether there are any dreams they remember. The dreams that are reported in response might not necessarily be initial dreams, dreamt just before the therapy started, but might be particularly powerful or recurrent dreams that will often have a particular importance for the dreamer and the course of the therapy.

Personally, I do not elicit dreams in this way, as I do not want to interfere with what people tell me (would they come to think that I particularly wanted them to tell me their dreams and would feel bad if they did not bring them, or would they unconsciously try to please me by bringing them?). I find that people usually tell me dreams in their own good time. Quite frequently, in the first few sessions, people will volunteer a dream they have had in the previous few days and it will turn out to be particularly resonant and informative.

CHAPTER ELEVEN

The Wolf-Man's dream: contrasting Freudian and Jungian approaches

S erguei Constantinovitch Pankejeff was twenty-three years old when he consulted Freud. Due to the dream that is analysed below he became known as "the Wolf-Man". He had become depressed after contracting gonorrhoea when he was eighteen and his depression had worsened after his father committed suicide when Serguei was nineteen and then worsened further when his sister also committed suicide two years later. He had become incapacitated and was completely dependent upon other people, so that he could not travel anywhere on his own and was constantly accompanied by a manservant and his personal physician. He had consulted many eminent physicians, who had not been able to help him, before he consulted Freud in February 1910, who immediately began an analysis with him (this account is taken largely from Quinodoz, 2005, pp. 156 ff.).

Serguei had been brought up in a wealthy aristocratic Russian family. He had been a good-natured boy, but he changed following the arrival of an English governess when he was three and a half years old (who was described as "eccentric", "quarrelsome", and "addicted to drink", and was clearly also cruel, openly calling Serguei's beloved, faithful nanny "a witch"), and also following his sister's sexual "playing" with him that occurred around that time (she was two years older than him); he became irritable, violent, and sadistic towards those close to him and towards animals. This behaviour changed again after a dream he had at the age of four, following which he developed a phobia of wolves and of other animals; the phobias subsided at the age of eight. This was his dream:

> It was night and I was lying in my bed. (My bed stood with its foot towards the window; in front of the window there was a row of old walnut trees. I knew it was winter when I had the dream, and night-time.) Suddenly the window opened of its own accord, and I was terrified to see that some white wolves were sitting on the big walnut tree in front of the window. There were six or seven of them. The wolves were white, and looked more like foxes or sheep-dogs, for they had big tails like foxes and they had their ears pricked like dogs when they pay attention to something. In great terror, evidently of being eaten up by the wolves, I screamed and woke up. [Freud, 1918b, p. 29]

His associations were as follows: the wolves being white reminded him of his father's large flocks of sheep that he sometimes visited with his father, at which times he felt proud and blissful, although once an epidemic had broken out and a vet had been called who gave them injections, but the sheep got worse and died. The wolves themselves, sitting in a tree, reminded him of three fairy tales: one where a tailor pulls off a wolf's tail and hides up a tree—he escapes being eaten by a pack of wolves that come after him by reminding the one wolf of his missing tail; the second was the Little Red Riding Hood story, where the wolf eats up Little Red Riding Hood's grandmother, disguises himself as the grandmother, and lies in wait for Red Riding Hood, but is eventually killed by a woodsman; the third was a tale where six out of seven goats are eaten up by a wolf, while the seventh escapes—the wolf finally perishes. He also associated the walnut tree to a Christmas tree, with the wolves sitting in it like presents (the dream was dreamt shortly before Christmas). He said the wolves were absolutely still and they had a strained attention as they all looked at him.

Freud worked on this dream with his patient for a number of years, with the interpretation only gradually emerging. Freud believed the wolves were father surrogates and said that Serguei was very afraid of his father. Freud held that the dream reminded him of something that had happened earlier in his life. From Serguei's associations to the fairy tales, Freud concluded that he had a fear of castration, symbolized by the association to the fairytale where the tail of the wolf was removed by the tailor.

Freud interpreted the strained attention of the wolves as the young boy's strained attention to something that Freud concludes was an observation of his parents having sex (the primal scene). He suggests the window opening was like the young Serguei's eyes opening, and that there was a reversal whereby, while the wolves in the dream were immobile, in fact there would have been violent motion in the scene of his parents having intercourse. Freud suggests his parents were having sex from behind and that he would have been able to observe their genitals and linked this to the wolves' tails hanging down.

Freud's interpretation was that the dream was a deferred reaction to this primal scene. Serguei's anxiety, he suggests, was due to a disguised and repressed wish for sexual satisfaction from his father, in the same manner as he had witnessed, which would require an identification with his mother, whom he had observed not to have male genitals and whom he would, therefore, have assumed had been castrated. In Freud's own words:

> His anxiety was a repudiation of the wish for sexual satisfaction from his father—the trend which had put the dream into his head. The form taken by the anxiety, the fear of "being eaten by the wolf" was only the . . . transposition of the wish to be copulated with by his father, that is, in the same way as his mother. His last sexual aim, the passive attitude toward his father, succumbed to repression, and fear of his father appeared in its place in the shape of the wolf phobia. [*ibid.*, p. 46]

Freud reasoned that Serguei's current passivity and incapacitation represented a return of this passive attitude toward his father.

A Jungian interpretation

In contrast, a possible Jungian interpretation might go as follows, assuming that there is no disguise in the dream, no reversal, and taking into account the dreamer's situation at the time of the dream. The dream could be understood to follow from the arrival of the English governess and his sister's sexual "playing" with him, at which point Serguei's personality had changed from good-natured to irritable, violent, and sadistic. We might assume that the new governess, her treatment of his nanny, and his sister's treatment of him, had brought about this change. However, this new, violent, sadistic behaviour was, presumably, unwelcome.

In this interpretation, the wolves represent the young Serguei's aggression, which he realizes is getting him into trouble. The dream offers a different, compensatory attitude to his conscious aggressive attitude (after the dream he is no longer sadistic and violent but becomes, instead, anxious and frightened of wolves and other animals). The wolves are in a tree opposite his (upper floor) window, they represent his aggression transposed into the head level (perhaps they mark his becoming properly conscious of his aggression, the windows, his eyes, becoming spontaneously open).

The wolves are also associated with a threat of castration (the tails can be removed)—a punishment for being bad and aggressive—and might also carry an element of sexual aggression, "wolfishness", related to his sister's sexual "play". The wolves in the tree are still—his aggression has been stilled; he has externalized his aggression into the wolves. The wolves look like sheepdogs in the way they attend to things (he has become attentive to his aggression), and are white like sheep; sheepdogs also keep things in order (sheep / feelings) and ward off wolves. The white ("good"?) sheep are associated with pleasant visits with his father and a feeling of security and peace—feeling in identification with him? Perhaps his aggression becoming stilled and turned "white" might be a kind of Christmas present to him and his parents, and might also have meant that he might receive Christmas presents (being well-behaved again).

He has become sheep-like, rather than wolf-like, a passive follower rather than a wild, sadistic, out of control force. However, even docile sheep are subject to threat, since the person called in to help them, the vet, seemed to cause further harm (he experienced extreme anxiety following the shift from wolf-likeness to sheep-likeness—he has exchanged aggression for anxiety). Seeing that the associations to the sheep, which include the vet memory, are current, we might speculate whether Freud might be seen as a current-day "vet" whose treatment he feared might make things worse.

Serguei became dissociated from his aggressive, sexual, wolf-like, life force and became "castrated". While he awoke to a fear of being

devoured by the wolves (he had become fully conscious of being swal-
lowed up by his aggression), at the time of the analysis with Freud he
had fallen back into passivity. We could suggest that his task in therapy would be to reconnect to his wolf-like aggression, to make it
manageable and integrate it. He had, perhaps, become like the wolf in
the Little Red Riding Hood story that was still a wolf, but dressed up
in grandma's clothes. He had now separated himself from the aggression, however, and was afraid of it wherever he saw it "out there"—
he had projected it into wolves, his father, and perhaps also the world
(seeing as he had become incapacitated and afraid).

While Freud termed his initial analysis of Sergueï a success, it is
generally agreed that he had only dealt with "the infantile neurosis"
and that Sergueï's underlying psychotic conflict had not been
addressed. Sergueï broke down again; the fact that he had lost all his
wealth in the Russian Revolution and lived the rest of his life in very
straitened means, relying, in fact, on Freud and his colleagues for
financial help, might have been another factor in his struggles. He
entered a further period of analysis with a different analyst, Ruth
Mack Brunswick, who specialized in working with psychosis; there he
made good further progress, Quinodoz reports (2005, p. 163).

Could both interpretations be true? It is entirely possible that
Sergueï had indeed observed the primal scene and feared castration,
as well as wanting to be passively loved by, and identified with, his
father, perhaps as a way of becoming potent again, without the danger
of having to embody his own aggression and potency. It is also possible that he felt he had witnessed a violent scene between his parents
and had tried to institute this elsewhere, attempting to dominate
others with his aggression, but this identification with his father had
failed and he had become passive (at the time of the dream), with his
own sense of potency and agency collapsing. It is striking that his
depression and helplessness had increased when both his father and
sister had committed suicide (his sister also used to taunt him with
pictures of wolves as a child); perhaps it was when these external
"containers" of his aggression had (aggressively) killed themselves
that his aversion to his own aggression—aggression which could have
increased his sense of self-agency—became stronger.

We might argue, therefore, that both dream interpretations could
be correct concerning this complex young man, as both reflect different aspects of his experience, related first to his aggression and second

to an early experience of observing the primal scene. I am struck, however, that much of Freud's interpretation of the dream follows from a series of associations over a period of years, and I would argue, therefore, following Jung's criticism of Freud's use of free association for dreams (see Chapter Three), that the Jungian-style interpretation stays closer to the dream itself.

I think the case for "reversal" in dreams is not proven: for example, "the wolves were still, therefore this relates to a scene where there was violent motion"; furthermore, I think it is precisely the dismissal of whole aspects of the dreamer's own personality, in this case his aggression, that leads to breakdown, severe psychopathology, and psychosis, rather than seeing this simply as repression due to conflict about his desire for sexual passivity and fear of castration.

It is noteworthy that one of Freud's intentions in describing his work with Sergueï was to refute Jung's criticisms of his work (which Freud called "twisted re-interpretations" of psychoanalysis (Freud, 1918b, p. 6, fn)) and, specifically, Jung's view of neurosis, which was that the current neurotic conflict arises from "a turning away from reality", "a substitutive satisfaction obtained in phantasy", and a regression to infantile states of mind; Freud wanted to demonstrate the centrality of infantile sexuality in the formation of the neurosis itself (*ibid.*, p. 53).

My "contemporary" Jungian interpretation, deriving specifically from Jung's form of dream interpretation, does take as its starting point the conflicts in Sergueï's infancy, in particular his aggression, but emphasizes much more their interpersonal origins (the arrival of the governess, her character, and his sister's sexual "play"), influences (Sergueï's situation in the family), and effects (his passivity and loss of self-agency in respect to others), rather than specifically sexual drives and conflicts (see also Knox, 2011, p. 21 for a discussion of the effect of actual trauma in relation to the Wolf-Man and his dream).

different of view on neurosis

Recent developments in understanding dreams and dreaming: dream laboratories and the neuroscience of dreams

As outlined in Chapter One, Aserinsky and Kleitman's identification of rapid eye movement (REM) sleep began a shift away from the interest in the content of dreams and a move towards an interest in their form and function. This shift became focused on the work of J. Allan Hobson and Robert McCarley, which gained substantial popular notoriety, with their reciprocal interaction and activation–synthesis models of dreaming (Hobson & McCarley, 1975, 1977), although these theories were much less taken up in the sleep research community itself (Domhoff, 2005).

The activation–synthesis model followed from the recognition that all mammals have periods of REM sleep, which Michel Jouvet investigated by removing parts of the brains of cats until he discovered that removal of a primitive and central part of the brain stem, known as the pons, prevented REM sleep. This led him to conclude that the pons was responsible for dreaming (Jouvet, 1962), while the higher mechanisms of the brain appeared to play little part. REM sleep was taken to be the neurophysiological counterpart of dreaming.

Hobson and McCarley's theory, building on Jouvet's discovery, was that REM sleep was "switched on" by a small group of cells in the pons excreting acetylcholine, the chemical responsible for attention, learning, and memory in the brain. This stimulus from the primitive part of the brain, they hypothesized, *activates* the higher parts of the brain which generate intrinsically meaningless conscious images, which are then *synthesized* into the narrative of the dream: in other words, it is a theory of activation and synthesis. The dream images are the higher brain "making the best of a bad job . . . from the noisy signals sent up to it from the brainstem" (Hobson & McCarley, 1977, p. 1347). We are back in the territory, familiar to Freud, of dreams being seen as "mere froth".

Their theory continued, identifying the mechanism by which this cholinergic activation was "switched off", which was through the counter-activation of another group of cells in the pons excreting nora-drenalin (responsible for physical and mental arousal and heightened mood) and serotonin (responsible for mood, emotion, and anxiety). Hobson and McCarley wrote, "If consciousness is in the forebrain we can completely eliminate any possible contribution of ideas to dream-ing" (*ibid.*, p. 1343).

While Hobson and McCarley have had to modify their argument and conclusions somewhat over time, recognizing that dreams do have personal meaning and reflect the personality and preoccupations of the dreamer, as I describe further below, their position is still far from recognizing the intricate significance of dreams that this book, for example, outlines. Furthermore, the tenor of the debate was bitter and sometimes mocking (no doubt careers and livelihoods were felt to depend on it, as a great deal of money was available for dream research at the time, since it was hoped that it would offer an insight into psychosis). Hobson, for example, writes, as late as 2005,

> Freud, like his followers, religiously believed that dream bizarreness was a psychological defence against an unacceptable unconscious wish. This seemed unlikely to many people in 1900. At the beginning of the twenty-first Century, it seems impossible to us. [Hobson, 2005, pp. 5–6]

and even, "The best that poor old Freud could do with flying dreams was to argue that they represented displaced sexual desire" (*ibid.*, p. 28)—"poor old Freud"?!

Before I come to this debate, and to Mark Solms' detailed rebuttal of Hobson and McCarley's position, I would like to look at some of what has been established about dreams and dreaming over the years by dream researchers and neuroscientists.

Three kinds of dreaming

Sleep and dreaming is a peculiar and particular state of mind and consciousness, where the mind–brain is, in fact, quite active.

1. As we drift off to sleep we quickly enter into "sleep-onset" dreams (people woken during this period report dreams 50–70% of the time); these are typically stimulated by an internal percept, for example: "I could feel myself moving just the way the sea moved our boat when I was out fishing today" (Hobson, 2005, p. 7).

2. REM sleep occurs periodically in ninety-minute cycles, occupying about a quarter of sleeping time. It is characterized by a burst of rapid eye movement, increased brain activation, increased breathing and heart rate, genital engorgement, and paralysis of bodily movement.

    Dreams frequently occur during this period—individuals woken during this time report dreams 90–95% of the time. REM dreams are generally dramatic, complex, bizarre, and longer than non-REM dreams (see below). There is vivid perception that often does not accord with reality—Hobson calls it hallucinatory and delusional.[1] An example (this is only one portion of the whole dream):

    > I am perched on a steep mountaintop; the void falls away to the left. As the climbing party rounds the trail to the right, I am suddenly on a bicycle, which I steer through the climbers. It becomes clear that I make a complete circuit of the peak (at this level) by staying on the grass. There is, in fact, a manicured lawn surface continuing between rocks and crags. [Hobson, 2005, p. 7]

3. Non-REM sleep and dreams intersperse periods of REM sleep. If individuals are woken during this state, they report "typical", in other words, REM style, dreams 5–10% of the time. However, when they were asked what was passing through their minds (rather than what they were dreaming), they describe mental activity about 50% of the time, although it tended to be more

similar to everyday thinking (Foulkes, 1962); there is no perception or hallucinatory aspect to this mental state, although there is
typically emotion. An example:

> I kept thinking about my upcoming exam and about the subject
> matter it will contain. I didn't sleep well because I kept waking up
> and was inevitably pulled back to the same ruminations about my
> exam. [Hobson, 2005, p. 7]

As the night goes on, non-REM dreams take on more of the characteristics of REM sleep, sometimes known as Stage II NREM
dreams (Antrobus, Kondo, & Reinsel, 1995, cited in Domhoff,
2005).

Criticisms of Hobson and McCarley's activation–synthesis model

Once it had been established that dreaming does occur in non-REM
sleep, the crude identification of REM sleep as the psycho-biological
correlate of dreaming was broken. Furthermore, Solms, working from
within the Freudian tradition, has challenged the basic tenets of their
theory and established that, while the destruction of the pons in cats
brought about the cessation of dreaming, it did not necessarily do so
in humans—only one in twenty-six individuals who had suffered
brain damage to the pons no longer dreamt.

In fact, Solms discovered that the cessation of dreaming occurred
where individuals had received injury and damage to three areas of
the brain, which he proposed, therefore, were necessary for dreaming:

1.   The white matter in the frontal lobes, which contains a large fibre
     pathway which transmits dopamine from the mid brain to the
     higher brain. Dopamine is responsible for arousal and the indi-
     vidual's curiosity–interest–expectancy responses, and this area
     instigates "goal seeking behaviour and the organism's appetitive
     interactions with the world" (Panksepp, 1985, p. 273, quoted in
     Solms, 2007).

     Solms is quick to point out that this dopamine pathway could
     be very much related to Freud's view that dreams are attempted
     wish-fulfilments, although this function could also be seen to be
     involved in motivation, interest, and orientation of the individual
     regarding their personal interests and concerns.

2. A portion of the grey cortex at the back of the brain (just behind and above the ears) called the occipito–temporo–parietal junction. This is responsible for the highest levels of processing of perceptual information, essential for "conversion of concrete perception into abstract thinking, and for memorizing of organized experience or, in other words, not only for the perception of information but its storage" (Luria, 1973, p. 74, cited in Solms, 2007 p. 149).

    This is the function that I described in Chapter Four as essential for the classification and processing of experience.

3. The right parietal lobe, affecting visual–spatial working memory (Kaplan-Solms & Solms, 2000), in other words, a part essential to perception and memory.

Solms, therefore, concluded that it was the *higher* functions of the brain that were essentially involved in dreaming and that, contrary to Hobson and McCarley's theory, destruction of the pons did not prevent dreams from occurring. Although in normal functioning the lower brain does play a role in dreaming, it is not even thought to be the trigger for dreaming (Solms, 1997, cited in Domhoff, 2001); furthermore, the brain stem (including the pons) is seen as more ordered than Hobson and McCarley hold (Jones, 2000) and to be in dynamic interaction with the higher-functioning frontal cortex (Siegal, 2000, cited in Domhoff, 2005).

Solms felt he had very much put the Freudian wish-fulfilment model back on the map, although he conceded then that he had not been able to identify the censoring function that Freud proposed, and that has been so much criticized. Domhoff has concluded, from the evidence of tens of thousands of dreams, that dream content in general is continuous with waking conceptions and emotional preoccupations (Domhoff, 2001, p. 13) and that dreams reflect or express more than they disguise (Domhoff, 2004, p. 12). I would suggest that the bizarreness and apparent disguise can be accounted for by the complex process of association related to symbol formation, as described in the earlier chapters of this book (see also Chapter Fourteen for Meltzer's parallel criticism of wish-fulfilment).

For their part, McCarley (1998) later acknowledges that dreams do have personal meaning and reflect the personality and preoccupations of the dreamer, while Hobson recognizes other functions (see below), although he emphasizes the essentially emotional nature and role of dreaming (common to both REM and non-REM dreams); as he puts it, "ignore the bizarreness and attend to the undisguised emotional content" (Hobson, 1999, p. 137; quoted in Wilkinson, 2006); although in fact approximately 25% of dreams are found not to be directly associated with affect (Fosse, Stickgold, & Hobson, 2001; Foulkes, Sullivan, Kerr, & Brown, 1988; Hall, 1951; Staunch & Meir, 1996, cited in Domhoff, 2005, p. 13).[2] Hobson's explanation for the bizarreness relies on what he calls the "hyperassociative" nature of dreaming, a concept he borrows from the nineteenth century associationist, David Hartley (Hobson, 2005, p. 23).

I would strongly argue that not only are the associations that the sleeping mind makes meaningful, but that they are an example of the sleeping mind working to process new experience by comparing the new experience with old patterns of behaviour and experience and, also, working on those previously stored complex emotional states/patterns/internal working models (see further below). This function is carried out, in part, by the occipito–temporo–parietal junction, the symbol-making mechanism of the mind–brain that links the particular perception with a generalized principle through association and similarity. As Rebeiro puts it, dreams are "hyper-associative strings of fragmented memories that stimulate past events and future expectations" (Rebeiro, 2004, p. 1, quoted in Wilkinson, 2006).

Domhoff, speaking from a cognitive theorist perspective, is critical of both Solms and Hobson and McCarley. He argues that there is no evidence that dreams represent attempted wish-fulfilments, attempts at dream disguise, or attempts to protect sleep, contra Solms and the Freudian position, or that dreams are meaningless froth, or are primarily expressions of affect, contra Hobson. His "neurocognitive theory of dreams" argues that dreams reflect waking conceptions and emotional preoccupations and are a developmental cognitive achievement that demonstrate, in their content, a significant continuity and repetition of themes (Domhoff, 2001). I think Hobson is correct to emphasize the role of affect in dreaming; however, I think he is mistaken in dismissing and downplaying the content of dreams, which, I believe, complements the affect; only together can there be a full picture (see below and Chapter Fourteen).

The functions of dreaming

The overall process of dreaming is now understood to be one where there is a reversal of the normal system of perception, so that external perception (sight, sound, taste, touch, and smell) is switched off, while dream imagery is generated by "projecting information backward in the system" (Kosslyn, 1994, p. 74), so that internally generated images are fed backwards into the cortex as if they were coming from outside (Zeki, 1993, p. 326, both quoted in Solms, 2007). Because of the suspension of the discriminating, rational functioning of the frontal cortex, the images/experiences that are generated by the dreaming mind–brain are accepted as real (sometimes we are not sure whether something really happened or whether we dreamt it[3]); importantly, however, because of the bodily paralysis, the images/experiences are not acted upon physically—we go on a psychic–emotional journey only.

One of the results of this process of dreaming is "the affective organisation of memory" (Reiser, 1999, p. 203, cited in Wilkinson, 2006, p. 138). Panksepp argues that REM sleep permits information processing, whereby transient memory stores become integrated into subconscious behavioural habits (Panksepp 1998, p. 129). He writes that REM sleep may help:

> to solidify the many unconscious habits that are the very foundation of our personality. In the final accounting dreams may construct the powerful subconscious or preconscious affective psychological patterns that make us . . . the people that we are. They may help construct the many emotional myths and beliefs around which our lives revolve. [Panksepp, 1998, p. 142, quoted in Wilkinson, 2006, p. 139]

These "subconscious or preconscious affective psychological patterns" are the internal working models (Bowlby) and ways of being with others (Stern) that I have described in this book. Dreaming can be understood, therefore, to be the processing of our experience, from the day and beyond, particularly our emotional experience; this processing stores and integrates that experience within our memory and with our sense of ourselves.

So, the dream (fragment) of meeting my uncle unexpectedly (Chapter Three) would be processing the concern about trust in relationships, associated with the newly begun counselling. This concern is "projected backwards" through the perceptual–experiential system, thus generating a particular dream image/symbol—meeting my uncle. The dream is an expression of the dreamer's work on this issue, establishing, unconsciously, a sense of trust in the new counsellor and working on the established pattern of a lack of trust in others.

As Rebeiro puts it, "the function of dreams is to trim and shape the memories acquired during waking, in a cyclic process of creation, selection and generalization of conjectures about the world" (Rebeiro, 2004, p. 12, quoted in Wilkinson, 2006, p. 132). Far from being meaningless mental processes, therefore, dreaming is a developmental achievement which allows better processing of experience (the dreams of children are much less frequent and much less sophisticated (Domhoff, 2001; Foulkes, 1982, 1999)).[4]

Even Hobson has come to recognize the value of dreaming in developing a secure sense of agency, as the "I" integrates the different experiences, senses of self, and, I would add, challenges presented in the dream (Hobson, 2005, pp. 64–68). He concludes that dreaming reveals "progressive, adaptive information processing during sleep" . . . the brain is always more active than not . . . processing information, consolidating and revising memory, and learning newly acquired skills" (pp. 141–142).

Sometimes, this unconscious process of dreaming becomes conscious, particularly when the sleeping mind cannot cope with or properly deal with the issues concerned, and we need to do active conscious work with the dream and its content.

Notes

1. Domhoff reports that only 9% of REM dreams are properly bizarre, with the rest found more to reflect waking life (Domhoff, 2005, p. 10), although I would question whether he is defining "bizarre" as "impossible", as almost all REM dreams contain some "slippage" from reality due to the process of symbolization and association.

2. It is important to note that while a dream might not have a particular emotional tone associated with it, the content of a dream will refer to an emotional preoccupation in some way or other, for example, the dream of "meeting my uncle" concerns the issue of trust, a matter of vital emotional importance; this point was made long ago by Freud (1900a, Chapter 6 (b)).

3. It is no doubt important that we do not remember *all* our dreams, other-
    wise we would be flooded by a whole lot more emotional experience that
    we would have to process, in other words we would have to do a lot
    more conscious work on what is essentially a system of unconscious
    processing; the forgetting of dreams is an important aspect of the dream
    system (Hobson, 2005, pp. 55 ff.).

4. Contrary to the popular modern belief that we all dream (although most
    people woken in REM sleep discover that they are dreaming even if they
    are not generally able to remember their dreams on waking), there
    are certain people (who do not have brain injury) who have "low visuo-
    spatial skills" who do not dream (Foulkes, 1982, 1999). Visual–spatial
    skills are vital for the inner perception that is characteristic of REM type
    dreaming.

CHAPTER THIRTEEN

Other dreams

Repetitive traumatic dreams

Repetitive dreams, which relive and replay particular traumas in the individual's life, were the one set of dreams that Freud recognized did not fit into his theory of wish-fulfilment (Freud, 1923c, p. 117). He thought that those who experienced such dreams were suffering from what he called traumatic neurosis, although we would now understand this as post traumatic stress disorder (PTSD). PTSD can be brought about by experiences of war, torture, accident, or physical, sexual, or emotional abuse, either as a child or as an adult.

In essence, the individual's psyche has not been able to bear or contain such experiences; in particular, it has not been able to integrate them with the individual's previous personality (ego) structure (this accounts for the fact that each individual has their own particular reaction to traumatic situations). A traumatic complex has been set up which centres around the traumatic experience and, as with all complexes, has a powerful affective (emotional) component which generates thoughts, feelings, dreams, or physical sensations (including "symptoms" of illness) and interferes with the individual's normal ego-functioning.[1] The dreams tend to be repetitive and simply replay and relive the original traumatizing experience, with little variation or progression. At the very least, such dreams demand the individual's attention and, ideally, alerts them to the possible need to seek assistance.[2]

Working with such traumas, and the dreams that accompany them, requires that a secure therapeutic relationship is established which allows the unfolding and judicious exploration of the traumatic experience. I say judicious, as care must be taken that exploring the trauma is not simply retraumatizing for the individual. Sometimes, active work needs to be undertaken to ensure that the experiences are remembered and re-experienced in a setting where they can be contained, borne, thought about, and worked through, rather than simply overwhelming the individual once again.[3]

Wilkinson describes her work with her client, "Susan", who experienced the early relational trauma of prolonged separation from her mother and abuse from an uncle. In her therapy, she brought the following dream:

> She was trying to escape from a young, dark-haired man who was in pursuit of her. She had a child with her. There were long corridors, perhaps a hospital environment, perhaps a school. She was surrounded by lots of people whose faces were very alive but who behaved as spectators, neither helping nor harming.

Susan contrasted this dream with her childhood repetitive nightmare. This adult dream was in colour and peopled, in contrast to the childhood nightmare, in which she fled alone down dark subterranean passages, or across dark, lonely landscapes (Wilkinson, 2006, p. 144).

In the adult dream, she was carrying the child, as opposed to *being* the child running away; this would indicate some development and perspective on her vulnerable childhood self and the presence of her adult ego that could help look after that child self, although her adult dream ego was also being pursued/threatened by the dark-haired man. The bleak empty corridors of the repetitive childhood nightmares suggest the absence of people to protect her, perhaps reflecting her prolonged separation from her mother. Wilkinson reports that, years later, Susan found a photograph of the uncle who had abused her, and he bore a striking resemblance to the dark-haired man who was chasing her in her dreams.

Nightmares

Such dreams are different from the nightmares that we all experience from time to time (even though there is some similarity and nightmares can reflect early relational trauma, they are not so unchangingly repetitive and are less debilitating). In nightmares, the negative affects and content are intense, shocking, horrific and/or terrifying, and frequently result in the dreamer waking in the midst of the nightmare.[4] Ogden (2004) describes nightmares as "interrupted dreams", in other words, dreams that could not be completed due to the power of the affects.

Studies of the content of dreams from a statistical point of view have shown that dreams with negative affects are more common than dreams with positive affects (Domhoff, 2001). This may well be because we naturally attempt to establish our lives in a positive framework, preferring good experiences over bad, so that negative experiences will be more disturbing and difficult and will require more dream work in order to integrate them. It is a significant developmental achievement when we are able to bear experiences of frustration, embarrassment, shame, and other such "negative" affects, and find a place for those experiences within ourselves; in other words, when we are able to integrate them with our ego.

It is important, however, to recognize the symbolic nature of such nightmares, where the threat is frequently from a disavowed part of the dreamer that appears to threaten the way the person sees him/herself in a fundamental way. Quinodoz points out that such dreams frequently occur at a time of integration, and suggests that they demonstrate that the client "is now able to accept hitherto unrepresentable parts of himself" (Quinodoz, 1999, p. 225).

Peters describes a recurrent nightmare of his patient, Mrs X (Peters, 1990, pp. 161–162), which follows the pattern that Quinodoz describes. Mrs X's nightmares started in different ways, but as soon as she found herself on a certain terrible street, the dream would take on a familiar pattern.

> She became aware that something or a lot of somethings were behind her. In some spooky way they seemed to be tied to her, so that run and run as she might, she could never escape them. The sense of them always behind her filled her with dread and terror, until she could breathe no more and

[Handwritten margin note: "Issue For utility" with additional illegible annotation]

run no more and she knew they would catch her, at which point she would wake in a state of panic.

Peters describes how the understanding that gradually emerged in therapy was that the "things" she was trying to escape were her feelings of anger and hatred for her mother, who had been narcissistic and self-centred, needing to be recognized and thought well of, unable to tolerate criticism or anger.

A series of dreams followed in the therapy that showed how the anger began to be transformed. At first, she dreamt that she was driving in a car and turned, very scared, to see that it was on fire; then she dreamt that she was on a cliff and a cannon was next to her, firing down on a galleon, yet she was trying to ignore this; finally she dreamt of reaching out to touch someone (whom she later associated with her mother) and a swarm of bees flew up (*ibid.*, p. 163).

The first development was that she was able to identify the rage/fire that was at the back of her car, rather than there just being something unknown pursuing her; then the cannon was aggressively firing down on the galleon, which she associated with her mother, but she still did not want to recognize her angry attacks; finally, the bees which fly up from the contact with her mother symbolize something both potentially creative—honey and love[5]—as well as stinging and dangerous. Peters comments that the dreamer had been able to bring her hate and her love together; her experience of her mother had become more rounded and bearable as she had been able to recognize, own, bear, and digest her experiences of anger and hate toward her.

Beebe (2005) distinguishes three kinds of nightmare. The first, like those described above, where the dreamer is confronted with something they have to do, yet which they feel unprepared for; he gives the example of a recurrent nightmare of someone trying to break into the house, which he understands to refer to the need to recognize a particular aspect of the dreamer's own personality. The second, where the dreamer is suddenly made aware of the true nature of a situation that they had thought to be otherwise; he gives the example of someone recognizing the murderousness (cold, unfeeling rejectingness) of a would-be partner. The third, which he calls "the empathy dream", where the dreamer has typically been absorbed in themselves, and has a nightmare which can serve to put them in touch with someone else's experience; he gives the example of a man who dreamt he was dying and, very soon after, his brother-in-law's aunt died; the dream made real the feelings associated with her death that he might otherwise, typically, have overlooked.

Beebe's classification distinguishes nightmares where the primary focus is the subjective level (the conflict of accepting a part of yourself) and the objective level (recognizing something in the other), while the empathy dreams seem to be good examples of "unconscious work" being done. I would want to ask whether it is quite as clear-cut as he proposes and whether there might not have been, *in addition*, objective, real-world correlates for the dream of someone trying to break into the house (was there a particularly intrusive individual in the dreamer's early life?), and subjective correlates or significances to the murderous potential partner (does the dreamer have a tendency to be murderous himself, or to project his murderousness, or to be particularly sensitive to being killed off?). Similarly, Mrs X's nightmares, which Peters describes, will also probably have objective, transference, and archetypal manifestations.

Night terrors

Night terrors are "dreams that are not dreams", as Ogden puts it (2004, p. 858). Certain individuals, typically in childhood, experience prolonged periods of terrifying and disturbing night terrors where the child wakes, utterly overwhelmed with terror, experiencing the physical symptoms associated with terror—sweating, racing heart rate, and other panic symptoms—and it is very difficult for adults who come to their aid to comfort them, as the child usually does not recognize the parent and, on waking, often has little recollection of the whole event.

These night terrors are not associated with "bad dreams"/nightmares which take place in REM sleep: they are a different phenomenon. As Ogden writes,

> Both from a psychoanalytic point of view and from the point of view of brain-wave activity, the person having a night terror does not wake up from the experience nor does he fall back to sleep after being calmed (Daws, 1989). A person having night terrors is unable to view them from the perspective of waking life. In Bion's terms, night terrors are constituted of raw sense impressions related to emotional experience (beta-elements) which cannot be linked in the process of dreaming, thinking or storage as memory. The child having night terrors can only

*Low night terror
one solved*
↓

genuinely wake up when he is able to dream his undreamt dream.
[Ogden, 2004, p. 859]

Because of the difficulty settling the very distressed child, it is quite common for the doctor to be called and for some kind of sedative medication to be administered. In his paper, Ogden describes the therapist's task as one of attempting to generate conditions where the client can dream their previously undreamable dreams.

Recurring dreams

Themes will frequently recur in dreams over many years, whether they are themes of anxiety, loss, fear, or longing, or dreams which evoke a particular setting, but whose emotional content is obscure. Recurring dreams of a pleasant nature are less common. Sometimes, characters, and frequently places, will recur over many years, but when a whole dream scenario recurs, this clearly signifies that the issue of the dream still has not been resolved and further work needs to be done. The recurring nightmares that I have described above serve as good examples. One client described her recurring dreams as follows:

> I have a recurring dream of looking for my flat. Sometimes I am quite frantic to find it, sometimes I find it but know that I am going to have to move out, sometimes I dream of flats that I have found but lost again. It is always in London.

This recurring dream described the dreamer's attempts to properly "inhabit" a part of herself that felt very important—it was in the capital city. Sometimes, she achieved this state of linking up with her more "true self", sometimes, she lost it and was remembering it sadly, sometimes, she was trying to fathom how to regain contact with this elusive central part of herself.

Series of dreams, individuation, and a critique of Jung

Jung writes,

> An obscure dream, taken in isolation, can hardly ever be interpreted with any certainty. For this reason I attach little importance to the interpretation of single dreams. A relative degree of certainty is

reached only in the interpretation of a series of dreams, where the later dreams correct the mistakes we have made in handling those that went before. Also, the basic ideas and themes can be recognized much better in a dream-series . . . [Jung, 1934b, par. 322]

Jung (1944, 1964 pp. 58 ff.) and Peters (1990) describe a number of series of dreams which show the development of the personality of the dreamer; Jung sees this as the operation of the individuation process. The dreams themselves clearly play an important role in that process and underline the importance of dreams and dreaming.

Domhoff has criticized Jung's dream theory, saying that Jung emphasizes "a pattern of symbolic change toward greater personal integration" and insufficiently recognizes the repetition that takes place in dreams, sometimes across a whole lifetime (Domhoff, 2001, p. 24). While themes do recur, sometimes over decades, reflecting the nature of the individual's personality and patterns of interaction, there can be a great deal of difference between, for example, an anxiety dream (or indeed an instance of anxiety) before therapy, where the anxiety may be overwhelming, and after therapy (or even after decades of life experience), where the anxiety might be contained by the other developments in the personality.

The example given above of Mrs X's recurrent nightmares of being "pursued by something or somethings", and her development in terms of her recognition and ownership of her anger and hatred, are good examples. The themes of fear and aggression might be the same, but there is all the difference in the world between the experience of being pursued by one's own projected aggression and owning and directing one's aggression constructively. Jung would say that the archetypal disposition / affects have been humanized.

We do not lose our fear, aggression, anxiety, self-centredness, and so on over our lifetimes; we do, however, hopefully, come to know about, contain, and make constructive use of these characteristics and affects. The repetition in dreams that Domhoff is referring to follows from these elements of our personality and from the internal working models that give our personalities dynamic relational structure.

Words and voices in dreams

Words often have a particular significance in dreams as the (unconscious) mind is adept at wordplay, word substitution, and use of homophones (words that sound like each other) and rebuses (where a word is displayed as an image)—all these slippages are forms of association.

I particularly watch out, to give just one example, for images of eyes and islands in dreams, as damage to the "eye" might not only signify a problem with seeing clearly, but could very well indicate some damage to the "I". Similarly, islands ("I"-lands) in dreams will often tell us a good deal about the state of the individual and their relation to others—I have quite often found an "I"-land distant from the mainland or linked by a rickety bridge which seemed to symbolize well the degree to which the dreamer felt separate, independent, and isolated from others, or connected in only a "rickety" and unsafe manner.

Homophones quite often come into dreams:

> I was drinking a glass of wine but it tasted horrible and I wanted to spit it out.

Here, the dreamer associated the image of drinking "wine" with "whine", and recognized that she felt she was whining at the moment and could not "spit out" what she really wanted to say because she feared it was too horrible.

> I went to a great deal of trouble cooking my mother-in-law some kind of French fish, but I was very surprised when she did not like it.

The dreamer was puzzled about this until she realized that the French word for fish is *poisson*, which she associated with poison. She recognized just how poisonous she was feeling towards her mother-in-law, which explained to her why they were not getting on at the time.

Sometimes single words are given particular weight in a way that can sound curious, bizarre, or fantastical:

> In the dream I heard the word "Eggs!" spoken loudly and I knew that this was the meaning of life.

This was dreamt by a woman who was feeling deeply dissatisfied with her life and had fallen into a depression. On exploring her associations to "Eggs!", we recognized the role of fertility, fecundity, and her own family in her life, a role she had been undervaluing in comparison to her envious over-valuation of a stereotypical high-powered career.

It is all in the name

I have quite often been surprised to find the action of a client's dream taking place in a particular street in Brighton, which is often not specifically named at first but, when I enquire, turns out to be either West Street or Western Road (my surname is West). Such wordplay allows the dreamer to convey something of the therapeutic relationship—perhaps someone hiding on West Street, or shouting at someone there, or stuck in a *cul-de-sac* off Western Road, and so on: symbols which need little interpretation from me.

The therapist's name(s) quite frequently appears in dreams, often in some bastardized form, or with someone else with the same first name used to indicate the therapist.

> I was with this boy I knew from school called Mark something or other, I can't remember his surname now, he was pointing me in the wrong direction.

When the dreamer had few associations to the dream, I pointed out that the name Mark was quite similar to Marcus, and asked whether the dreamer felt I had been "pointing her in the wrong direction" recently.

A particular favourite of mine along these lines is from someone who told me a long and detailed dream about walking along a beach and going into a cafe, before adding that she thought the beach was West Wittering beach (a particularly fine beach along the South Coast of England). The dreamer and I explored whether her dream was suggesting that she felt I had been "wittering on"!

Numbers

Similarly, numbers frequently play an important role, with the number often symbolizing, for instance, the number of sessions per week, or the number of sessions left before a break, or the cost of the sessions. Sometimes, numbers refer to a house number that can give a clue to what is being symbolized—"I lived at number 52 when my parents separated"—or an event that took place at a certain age or a date. Jung reports a dream where a high number represented the financial cost that the dreamer reckoned a sexual affair had cost him;

while in another dream, a number represented the number of children that Jung had compared to the dreamer, alluding to the dreamer's envy of Jung (Jung, 1910–1911, par. 129 ff.). The dreamer's associations to the number, however obscure they might seem, are vital.

Oedipal issues of exclusion and jealousy are quite often flagged up if there are three people in a particular scene, or the number three appears in some form or another. Jung held that the number four, or squares, in dreams symbolized completeness in some way (referring, as he saw it, to the presence of all four functions of the personality—thinking, feeling, intuition, and sensation—or the four elements: earth, air, fire, water, and so on). Those with an interest in numerology sometimes explore the archetypal significance of numbers in dreams along these lines. The number seven, for example, is taken to be a sacred number, twelve is taken to relate to time (twelve months in the year/signs of the zodiac), and so on (see, for example, Jung, 1952, pars 870–871). I would caution against using the archetypal meanings of number as a first port of call and, as always, would suggest that personal associations take precedence, but this other level of meaning could give something of a clue, particularly if backed up by other indicators in a dream.

The therapist's own dream work

Finally, we come to the therapist's own dreams. When the therapist has finished their own therapy, dreams serve as the most illuminating, reliable, useful and, indeed, essential way of keeping in touch with what is really going on in ourselves and our lives, both for our own sake and for the sake of our work with our clients. Having said that, working with and understanding our own dreams is probably more difficult than working with a client's, as we each have our own blind spots and defences and, because we are working with our own self, there is not the distance between ourselves and the "subject matter" which might afford us more objectivity—two brains are better than one when it comes to dream interpretation. Freud's and Jung's self-analysis of their dreams are particularly good examples of this, as Jung, for example, often misses the personal and relational elements in his own dreams and, instead, preferences the general and archetypal themes.

Jung was aware of the difficulty of interpreting your own dreams; as he put it,

> I have noticed that dreams are as simple or as complicated as the dreamer is himself, only they are always a little bit ahead of the dreamer's consciousness. I do not understand my own dreams any better than any of you, for they are always somewhat beyond my grasp and I have the same trouble with them as anyone who knows nothing about dream interpretation. Knowledge is no advantage when it is a matter of one's own dreams. [Jung, 1935, par. 244]

Having said that, dreams are still able to give us the most honest and direct insight into ourselves. I have no particular "advice" on working with one's own dreams, other than saying that all I have said in this book about dreams also applies to our own dreams (obviously), and that we must each develop our own way of working with our dreams. It is particularly important, however, to find a way to allow space for the exploration stage of the dream analysis, unpacking the associations, rather than rushing to an interpretation.

Dreams about the client

A particular subset of the therapist's dreams are dreams about our clients. This raises a number of important issues, such as how much *are* they about the client, and should we consider telling the client the dream? Jung gives us a very good example of such a dream. He describes his client as an intelligent woman, yet in the therapy he noticed that increasingly there was a shallowness entering into their dialogue. He determined to speak to her about it and the night before the session he had the following dream:

> He was walking down a highway through a valley in late-afternoon sunlight. To his right was a steep hill. At its top stood a castle and on the highest tower was a woman sitting on a kind of balustrade. In order to see her properly he had to bend his head far back. He awoke with a crick in his neck. Even in the dream he had recognised the woman as his patient. [Jung, 1963, p. 155]

He saw this as a compensation dream; he felt that in the therapy he had been beginning to look down on his patient, but in the dream he is forced to correct this attitude and he had to look up to her, in other words, treat her with more respect. Jung told his patient the dream, and his interpretation of the dream, and he reports that "this produced an immediate change in the situation and the treatment once more began to move forward". This is an example of the way we are all the time processing information unconsciously, and that this can appear very helpfully in dreams regarding our therapeutic work, as a form of supervision.

Jung treats this dream primarily on the objective and transference levels (his transference towards his patient), and yet what does the dream also tell us about Jung and his attitudes in general—the subjective and archetypal levels? While, on the surface, a dream might appear to be referring to a particular situation with a particular client, it will also reveal a good deal about the therapist and their own conflicts. For example, why has the therapist's unconscious picked out this particular client to dream about, and why at this particular time? What particular issue or conflict is the client symbolizing for the therapist? We hear little about Jung's sister, and there is good reason to believe from Jung's own history that he undervalued both his wife and his mother, issues that could be thought to be revealed in this dream. Blechner also explores this subject, and he concludes that when you tell a client your dream, "you will be telling them much more than you realize" (2001, p. 225).

Furthermore, is it really necessary to tell the client in order to reap the benefit from the dream? I would suggest not. If the therapist discovers from their private exploration of the dream that they are looking down on their client, or afraid of their client, or can see that their client is in some way murderous or particularly vulnerable, then, in my experience, such knowledge can lead either to an automatic and natural change in the therapist's own attitude to the client (they begin treating them with more respect, or whatever), or the knowledge can be used to inform an interpretation of the issue when it next arises.

The dream can give new insight into the therapeutic relationship, but there is no reason to alter the normal therapeutic boundaries and for the therapist to make what amounts to a personal disclosure of the dream, even if it appears to be primarily about the client. Such a disclosure is an undigested communication that can have unforeseen consequences; for example, it can lead the client into unnecessary, distracting, and unhelpful speculation about the therapist's own conflicts. Equally, they might have a quite complex set of feelings about having learnt that the therapist was "looking down on them", as in Jung's case, even if it seems, at first, like "good news".

Notes

1. There is a clear link between dreaming and mental health; in the 1960s, Dement and Fisher conducted experiments on prolonged sleep deprivation (that would no longer be permitted, as they would be considered unethical and dangerous) that induced psychosis in some participants (Hobson, 2005, p. 72). More interesting, perhaps, is the finding that depressed patients who were deprived of a single night of REM dreaming experienced some relief from their depression (*ibid.*, p. 94); indeed, many depressed patients report feeling worse on first waking up. This would suggest that the individual has been immersed in the negatively-toned emotional/depressive complex and it takes some time to reconnect with other elements of their personality; the depressed emotional tone tends to lessen as the day goes on.

2. Jung (1948[1916], pars 499–502) also discusses such dreams, describing them as "reaction-dreams".

3. See Van der Hart, Nijenhuis, and Steele (2006) for an example of the kind of setting and work necessary to address trauma which has resulted in dissociation within the personality, where separate identities have been set up in order to deal with different aspects of the individual's traumatic experience, resulting in a dissociative identity disorder.

4. Peters (1990) points out that the term "nightmare" was originally used to refer to "a supernatural being, a spirit or monster or witch, typically female, that beset people in their sleep" (p. 157); the term reflects the ancient belief that dreams come upon us from an outside source.

5. Peters amplifies the dream by linking it to the myth of Aphrodite, the love-goddess, who was very much associated with bees; for example, at Aphrodite's temple at Eryx, in Sicily, priestesses were called "melissae", which means "bees", while Aphrodite herself was called Melissa, the queen bee.

CHAPTER FOURTEEN

Final thoughts:
twenty-first-century dreaming

I shall, finally, draw together some of the threads of this book, try to answer some of the questions left hanging from earlier chapters, and look at some of the quite radical issues both about dreams and what they tell us about the psyche. To start with, some of the more prosaic questions about Jung and Freud and how and whether we can, or should, reconcile the Jung-compensation *vs.* Freud-wish-fulfilment-disguise debate . . .

Meltzer (1983, p. 12) questions Freud's theory of wish-fulfilment, asking what is meant by "wish"—is it intention, motive, plan, desire, impulse, or expectation? Certainly, dreams do reflect the individual's wishes, hopes, fears, goals, personality, and preoccupations, and are, thus, powerfully related to our emotional life, relationships, and reality. Similarly, Jung's concept of compensation reflects the notion that the dream is adding something new to our understanding of ourselves; it is, therefore, purposeful and goal orientated. Both are attempted catch-all definitions which both over-stretch themselves in their attempt to be universal and very much reflect each theorist's views about what the primary motivating factors are in the psyche: wishes–impulses–drives for Freud, and the development of the personality for Jung.

As suggested in Chapter Three, Freud's and Jung's views on the primary motivation of the psyche are now somewhat dated, and there has been a far-reaching shift in our understanding of human nature and functioning. The shift has, I would suggest, subtly but profoundly altered our understanding of the value and role of dreams and dreaming; dreams themselves played a role in consolidating this new emphasis. This has come about primarily through our appreciation of the fundamental role of relationship in human development and human life, as well as an appreciation of the significance of emotion and its relation to thought (e.g., Bion, 1962; Damasio, 1994, 1999; Knox, 2003; LeDoux, 1996; Schore, 1994; Stern, 1985). Curiously, while the shift in the academic interest in dreams was moving from dream content to the form and function of dreams, so, in the psychoanalytic world, has there been a growing appreciation of the process of dreaming and the role of affect in the psyche.

Bion (1962) described the mother's essential role in helping the infant bear, contain, transform, and, ultimately, think about their experience. He understood that emotional experience, which he termed "beta elements", was primary in this process and constitutes our primary response to our environment. The individual then has to do active work/thinking—which he calls "alpha functioning", in order to transform these emotional experiences (beta elements) into alpha elements. No longer was feeling seen as something that got in the way of the "gold standard" of thinking (see also West, 2007, Chapter Three).

Following Bion, psychoanalysts like Meltzer (1983) and Ogden (1996, 2004, 2007) have recognized the importance of the process of dreaming, dominated as it is by emotion and association, in the life of the individual and as a part of the process of thinking and, therefore, development itself. As Meltzer puts it "dreaming is unconscious thinking". The development of the individual depends on their ability to know about their emotional life (words are married to the emotional experience); this knowledge represents an extension of the ego and is, therefore, a growth of the self.

Ogden has taken these notions further, and has explored the way that some elements of dreaming are present in, and vital to, waking life—essentially, the emotional linking and (free) association. He calls this "waking-dreaming", and also applies this to the practice of therapy with his notion of "talking-as-dreaming", where he notes that if individuals are not able to associate and emotionally link in this way, the therapeutic relationship, as well as the individuals them-selves, can become lifeless, the connection to the other is lost, and the individuals can lose themselves. Ogden suggests that, in a very real way, we "dream ourselves into being" by being emotionally present and connected to our experience and to others (Ogden, 2007, Chapter 2). Gus Cwik (2011) develops these ideas further from a contemporary Jungian position.

Ogden's recognition of these processes in waking life is, for me, saying a similar thing to Matte Blanco, as described in Chapter Four, about the role of affect and its relationship to forming links and asso-ciations (Ogden's theory uses Kleinian language, however). This kind of emotionally based associative linking is the bedrock of our func-tioning, both in waking life and in dreams. In dreaming, however, it comes to the fore, while in waking life it is going on in the back-ground. Personally, I do not see any great merit in extending the term "dreaming" to waking life, as Meltzer and Ogden propose (see West (2007) for an exploration of the constant background operation of this appraisal, assessment, association and linkage within us).

These psychoanalytic notions regarding the centrality of emotional experience and relationship have largely been underpinned by the findings of neuroscience, research from dream laboratories, and from infant development studies. These views also dovetail with, and develop, Jung's understanding of dreams and dreaming, which has provided the framework for this book. Jung's later definition of dreams as "a spontaneous self-portrayal, in symbolic form, of the actual situation in the unconscious" (Jung, 1948[1945], par. 505) comes very close to the contemporary position.

While each of these fields presents a different emphasis and, like dreams themselves, pare, trim, and reshape our current body of know-ledge, the confluence of the findings in the different fields is, to my mind, striking, particularly regarding the role of association, symbol-ization, and emotion. Those who like an argument and wish to emphasize the small differences between and within these fields will always find something to disagree about.

Exploring the associations to and around dream images and dream narratives, paying particular attention to the emotional links, is a simple, effective and illuminating way of understanding the symbolic nature of dreams and, thereby, of helping the individual to develop themselves, their relationships, and their lives in a fulfilling way.

I would suggest that dreams can, and ideally should, be considered on all the levels that Jung outlines—objective, subjective, transference, and archetypal levels: this opens up the full breadth of their symbolic meaning. I recognize that it is impractical to approach each and every dream in this way, as there are probably too many dreams and too much else requiring our limited attention (which is why we do so much processing when we are asleep, in dreams!). However, much can be gained from the exploration of particular dreams in this way, when and where it is called for, as I hope I have demonstrated in this book.

Dreams are the richest "source" available to us; they work on the emotional raw material of our life experience. Sometimes, we need to supplement this unconscious work with conscious exploration and analysis of certain dreams; this work keeps us vitally congruent with our true selves.

unprocessed   emotional   material   processed

*dream
in
general*

*Solms
et
Cours
emphasizing
on other function*

REFERENCES

Adams, M. V. (2001). *The Mythological Unconscious*. New York: Karnac.

Antrobus, J., Kondo, T., & Reinsel, R. (1995). Dreaming in the late morning: summation of REM and diurnal cortical activation. *Consciousness & Cognition*, 4: 275–299.

Aristotle (1941). On prophesying by dreams. In: R. McKeon (Ed.), *The Basic Works of Aristotle*. New York: Random House.

Astor, J. (2002). Analytical psychology and its relation to psychoanalysis: a personal view. *Journal of Analytical Psychology*, 47: 599–612.

Beebe, J. (2005). Finding our way in the dark. *Journal of Analytical Psychology*, 50(1): 91–101.

Bion, W. (1962). *Learning From Experience*. London: Heinemann.

Blechner, M. (2001). *The Dream Frontier*. Hillsdale, NJ: Analytic Press.

Bowlby, J. (1969). *Attachment and Loss, Vol. 1 Attachment*. London: Hogarth Press.

Bowlby, J. (1980). *Attachment and Loss, Vol. 3 Loss: Sadness & Depression*. London: Hogarth Press.

Cambray, J., & Carter, L. (2004). *Analytical Psychology: Contemporary Perspectives in Jungian Analysis*. Hove: Brunner-Routledge.

Clark, M. (2006). *Understanding the Self-Ego Relationship in Clinical Practice: Towards Individuation*. London: Karnac.

Colman, W. (2005). Sexual metaphor and the language of unconscious phantasy. *Journal of Analytical Psychology, 50*: 641–660.

Colman, W. (2010). Dream interpretation and the creation of symbolic meaning. In: M. Stein (Ed.), *Jungian Psychoanalysis* (pp. 94–108). Chicago, IL: Open Court.

Cwik, A. J. (2011). Associative dreaming: reverie and active imagination. *Journal of Analytical Psychology, 56*(1): 14–36.

Damasio, A. (1994). *Descartes' Error: Emotion, Reason and the Human Brain.* New York: HarperCollins.

Damasio, A. (1999). *The Feeling of What Happens: Body, Emotion and the Making of Consciousness.* London: Vintage.

Daws, D. (1989). *Through the Night: Helping Parents and Sleepless Infants.* London: Free Association Books.

Domhoff, G. W. (2001). A new neurocognitive theory of dreams. *Dreaming, 11*(1): 13–33.

Domhoff, G. W. (2004). Why did empirical dream researchers reject Freud? A critique of historical claims by Mark Solms. *Dreaming, 14*(1): 3–17.

Domhoff, G. W. (2005). Refocusing the neurocognitive approach to dreams: a critique of the Hobson versus Solms debate. *Dreaming, 5*(1): 3–20.

Edinger, E. F. (1972). *Ego and Archetype.* Boston, MA: Shambhala.

Fairbairn, W. R. D. (1940). Schizoid factors in the personality. In: *Psychoanalytic Studies of the Personality.* London: Routledge, 1952.

Fonagy, P., Gergely, G., Jurist, E., & Target, M. (2002). *Affect Regulation, Mentalization and the Development of the Self.* London: Karnac.

Fosse, R., Stickgold, R., & Hobson, J. A. (2001). The mind in REM sleep: reports of emotional experience. *Sleep, 24*: 947–955.

Foulkes, D. (1962). Dream reports from different states of sleep. *Journal of Abnormal and Normal Social Psychology, 65*: 14–25.

Foulkes, D. (1982). *Children's Dreams.* New York: Wiley.

Foulkes, D. (1999). *Children's Dreaming and the Development of Consciousness.* Cambridge, MA: Harvard University Press.

Foulkes, D., Sullivan, B., Kerr, N., & Brown, L. (1988). Appropriateness of dream feelings to dreamed situations. *Cognition and Emotion, 2*: 29–39.

Freud, S. (1900a). *The Interpretation of Dreams. S.E., 4–5.* London: Hogarth.

Freud, S. (1901a). On dreams. *S.E., 5*: 629–686. London: Hogarth.

Freud, S. (1915e). The unconscious. *S.E., 14*: 159–215. London: Hogarth.

Freud, S. (1918b). *From the History of an Infantile Neurosis* (the 'Wolf Man'). *S.E., 17*: 1–122. London: Hogarth.

Freud, S. (1923b). *The Ego and the Id. S.E., 19*: 1–66. London: Hogarth.

Freud, S. (1923c). Remarks on the theory and practice of dream interpretation. *S.E., 19*: 107–122. London: Hogarth.

Freud, S., & Breuer, J. (1895d). *Studies on Hysteria. S.E., 20.*

Hall, C. (1951). What people dream about. *Scientific American, 184*(5): 60–63.

Hall, J. A. (1983). *Jungian Dream Interpretation: A Handbook of Theory and Practice.* Toronto: Inner City Books.

Henderson, J. (1988). The cultural unconscious. *Quadrant, 21*(2): 7–16.

Hillman, J. (1979). *The Dream and the Underworld.* New York: Harper & Row.

Hillman, J. (1983). *Inter Views: Conversations Between James Hillman and Laura Pozzo on Therapy, Biography, Love, Soul, Dreams, Work, Imagination and the State of Culture.* New York: Harper & Row.

Hobson, J. A. (1999). The new neuropsychology of sleep: implications for psychoanalysis. *Neuropsychoanalysis, 1*(2): 157–183.

Hobson, J. A. (2005). *Dreaming: A Very Short Introduction.* Oxford: Oxford University Press.

Hobson, J. A., & McCarley, R. W. (1975). Neuronal excitability modulation over the sleep cycle: a structural and mathematical model. *Science, 189*: 58–60.

Hobson, J. A., & McCarley, R. W. (1977). The brain as a dream state generator: an activation-synthesis hypothesis of the dream process. *American Journal of Psychiatry, 134*: 1335–1348.

Jones, B. E. (2000). The interpretation of physiology. *Behavioural and Brain Sciences, 23*: 955–956.

Joseph, B. (1985). Transference: the total situation. *International Journal of Psychoanalysis, 66*: 447–454.

Jouvet, M. (1962). Recherches sur les structures nerveuses et les méchanismes responsables des differentes phases du sommeil physiologique. *Archives Italiennes de Biologie, 153*: 125–206.

Jung, C. G. (1909). The analysis of dreams. In: *Freud and Psychoanalysis,* R. F. C. Hull (Trans.). *C.W., 4.* London: Routledge & Kegan Paul.

Jung, C. G. (1910–1911). On the significance of number dreams. In: *Freud and Psychoanalysis,* R. F. C. Hull (Trans.). *C.W., 4.* London: Routledge & Kegan Paul.

Jung, C. G. (1911–1912). *Symbols of Transformation,* R. F. C. Hull (Trans.), *C.W., 5.* London: Routledge & Kegan Paul.

Jung, C. G. (1917). On the psychology of the unconscious. In: *Two Essays in Analytical Psychology,* R. F. C. Hull (Trans.). *C.W., 7.* London: Routledge & Kegan Paul.

Jung, C. G. (1921). *Psychological Types*, R. F. C. Hull (Trans.), *C.W.*, *6*. London: Routledge & Kegan Paul.

Jung, C. G. (1922). On the relation of analytical psychology to poetry. In: *The Spirit in Man, Art, and Literature*, R. F. C. Hull (Trans.). *C.W.*, *15*. London: Routledge & Kegan Paul.

Jung, C. G. (1926). Spirit and life. In: *The Structure and Dynamics of the Psyche*, R. F. C. Hull (Trans.). *C.W.*, *8*. London: Routledge & Kegan Paul.

Jung, C. G. (1928). The relations between the ego and the unconscious. In: *Two Essays on Analytical Psychology*, R. F. C. Hull (Trans.). *C.W.*, *7*. London: Routledge & Kegan Paul.

Jung, C. G. (1934a). The meaning of psychology for modern man. In: *Civilization in Transition*, R. F. C. Hull (Trans.). *C.W.*, *10*. London: Routledge & Kegan Paul.

Jung, C. G. (1934b). The practical use of dream-analysis. In: *The Practice of Psychotherapy*, R. F. C. Hull (Trans.). *C.W.*, *16*. London: Routledge & Kegan Paul.

Jung, C. G. (1935). The Tavistock Lectures. In: *The Symbolic Life*, R. F. C. Hull (Trans.). *C.W.*, *18*. London: Routledge & Kegan Paul.

Jung, C. G. (1944). *Psychology and Alchemy*, R. F. C. Hull (Trans.). *C.W.*, *12*. London: Routledge & Kegan Paul.

Jung, C. G. (1946). Analytical psychology and education. In: *The Development of Personality*, R. F. C. Hull (Trans.). *C.W.*, *17*. London: Routledge & Kegan Paul.

Jung, C. G. (1948)[1916]. General aspects of dream psychology. In: *The Structure and Dynamics of the Psyche*, R. F. C. Hull (Trans.). *C.W.*, *8*. London: Routledge & Kegan Paul.

Jung, C. G. (1948)[1945]. On the nature of dreams. In: *The Structure and Dynamics of the Psyche*, R. F. C. Hull (Trans.). *C.W.*, *8*. London: Routledge & Kegan Paul.

Jung, C. G. (1952). Synchronicity: an acausal connecting principle. In: *The Archetypes and the Collective Unconscious*, R. F. C. Hull (Trans.). *C.W.*, *8*. London: Routledge & Kegan Paul.

Jung, C. G. (1957). The Houston films, R. Evans (Ed.). In: W. McGuire & R. F. C. Hull, (Eds.), *C. G. Jung Speaking: Interviews and Encounters*, London: Picador, 1980.

Jung, C. G. (1963). *Memories, Dreams, Reflections*, A. Jaffé (Ed.). London: Collins.

Jung, C. G. (1964). *Man and his Symbols*. London: Picador.

Jung, C. G. (1984)[1938]. *The Seminars, Volume One, Dream Analysis: Notes from the Seminar Given in 1928–1930*. London: Routledge & Kegan Paul.

Kaplan-Solms, K., & Solms, M. (2000). *Clinical Studies in Neuropsycho-analysis: Introduction to a Depth Neuropsychology*. Madison, CT: International Universities Press.

Knox, J. (2003). *Archetype, Attachment, Analysis: Jungian Psychology and the Emergent Mind*. New York: Brunner-Routledge.

Knox, J. (2011). *Self-Agency in Psychotherapy: Attachment, Autonomy and Intimacy*. New York: Norton.

Kosslyn, S. (1994). *Image and Brain*. Cambridge, MA: MIT Press.

Kradin, R. (2006). *The Herald Dream: An Approach to Dream Interpretation and the Implications of Initial Dreams in Psychotherapy*. London: Karnac.

Kramer, M., Schoen, L., & Kinney, L. (1987). Nightmares in Vietnam veterans. *Journal of the American Academy of Psychoanalysis, 15*: 67–81.

Lakoff, G. (1977). How unconscious metaphorical thought shapes dreams. In: D. Stein (Ed.), *Cognitive Science and the Unconscious* (pp. 89–120). Washington, DC: American Psychiatric Press.

Lambert, K. (1981). *Analysis, Repair and Individuation*. London & New York: Academic Press.

Laplanche, J., & Pontalis, J.-B. (1973). *The Language of Psychoanalysis*. London: Karnac.

LeDoux, J. E. (1996). *The Emotional Brain: The Mysterious Underpinnings of Emotional Life*. New York: Simon & Schuster.

Luria, A. (1973). *The Working Brain*. Harmondsworth: Penguin.

Matte Blanco, I. (1975). *The Unconscious as Infinite Sets*. Maresfield Library. London: Karnac.

Matte Blanco, I. (1988). *Thinking, Feeling and Being*. London: Routledge.

McCarley, R. W. (1998). Dreams: disguise of forbidden wishes or transparent reflections of a distinct brain state? *Annals of the New York Academy of Science 1998 May 15; 843*: 116–133.

Meltzer, D. (1983). *Dream-Life*. Strathtay, Perthshire: Clunie Press.

Ogden, T. H. (1996). Reconsidering three aspects of psychoanalytic technique. *International Journal of Psychoanalysis, 77*: 883–899.

Ogden, T. H. (2004). This art of psychoanalysis: dreaming undreamt dreams and interrupted cries. *International Journal of Psychoanalysis, 85*: 857–877.

Ogden, T. H. (2007). *Rediscovering Psychoanalysis: Thinking and Dreaming, Learning and Forgetting*. London: Routledge.

Palombo, S. (1984). Recovery of early memories associated with reported dream imagery. *American Journal of Psychiatry, 141*: 1508–1511.

Panksepp, J. (1985). Mood changes. In: P. Vinken, C. Bruyn, & H. Klawans (Eds.), *Handbook of Clinical Neurology, Vol. 45*. Amsterdam: Elsevier.

Panksepp, J. (1998). *Affective Neuroscience: The Foundations of Human and Animal Emotions*. New York: Oxford University Press.

Peters, R. (1990). *Living with Dreams*. London: Rider.

Quinodoz, J.-M. (1999). Dreams that turn over a page: integration dreams with paradoxical regressive content. *International Journal of Psycho-analysis*, *80*(2): 225–238.

Quinodoz, J.-M. (2005). *Reading Freud: A Chronological Exploration of Freud's Writings*. London: Routledge.

Rebeiro, S. (2004). Towards an evolutionary theory of sleep and dreams. *MultiCiência*, *3*: 1–20.

Reiser, M. F. (1999). Commentary on the new neuropsychology of sleep. *Neuropsychoanalysis*, *1*(2): 196–206.

Rosenfeld, H. R. (1971). A clinical approach to the psycho-analytic theory of the life and death instincts: an investigation into the aggressive aspects of narcissism. In: *Melanie Klein Today. Vol: 1, Mainly Theory*, E. Bott Spillius (Ed.). London: Routledge, 1988 [first published in *International Journal of Psychoanalysis*, *52*: 169–178].

Samuels, A., Shorter, B., & Plaut, F. (1986). *A Critical Dictionary of Jungian Analysis*. London & New York: Routledge.

Schore, A. N. (1994). *Affect Regulation and the Origin of the Self*. Hillsdale, NJ: Lawrence Erlbaum.

Siegal, J. (2000). Brainstem mechanisms generating REM sleep. In: M. Kryger, T. Roth, & W. Dement (Eds.), *Principles and Practices of Sleep Medicine* (3rd edn) (pp. 112–133). Philadelphia, PA: Saunders.

Solms, M. (1997). *The Neuropsychology of Dreams: A Clinico-anatomical Study*. Hillsdale, NJ: Erlbaum.

Solms, M. (2007). The interpretation of dreams and the neurosciences. In: L. Mayes, P. Fonagy, & M. Target (Eds.), *Developmental Science and Psychoanalysis: Integration and Innovation* (pp. 141–158). London: Karnac.

Solms, M., & Turnbull, O. (2002). *The Brain and the Inner World: An Intro-duction to the Neuroscience of Subjective Experience*. New York: Other Press.

Staunch, I., & Meier, B. (1996). *In Search of Dreams: Results of Experi-mental Dream Research*. Albany, NY: State University of New York Press.

Stern, D. N. (1985). *The Interpersonal World of the Infant* (revised 1998). New York: Basic Books.

Van der Hart, O., Nijenhuis, E., & Steele, K. (2006). *The Haunted Self: Structural Dissociation and the Treatment of Chronic Traumatization*. New York: W. W. Norton.

Von Franz, M. L. (1980). *Redemption Motifs in Fairytales*. Toronto: Inner City Books.

Waldhorn, H. F. (Reporter) (1967). *Indications for Psychoanalysis: the Place of the Dream in Clinical Psychoanalysis. Monograph II* of the Kris Study Group of the New York Psychoanalytic Institute, E. Joseph (Ed.). New York: International Universities Press.

Watson, J. S. (1994). Detection of self: the perfect algorithm. In: S. Parker, R. Mitchell, & M. Boccia (Eds.), *Self-Awareness in Animals and Humans: Developmental Perspectives* (pp. 131–149). New York: Cambridge University Press.

Watson, J. S. (1995). Self-orientation in early infancy: the general role of contingency and the specific case of reaching to the mouth. In: P. Rochat (Ed.), *The Self in Infancy: Theory and Research* (pp. 375–393). Amsterdam: Elsevier.

West, M. A. S. (2007). *Feeling, Being and the Sense of Self: A New Perspective on Identity Affect and the Narcissistic Disorders*. London: Karnac.

West, M. A. S. (2008). The narrow use of the term ego in analytical psychology: the 'not-I' is also who I am. *Journal of Analytical Psychology*, 53: 367–388.

Whitmont, E. C., & Perera, S. B. (1989). *Dreams, A Portal to the Source*. London: Routledge.

Wilkinson, M. (2006). *Coming into Mind: The Mind–Brain Relationship: A Jungian Clinical Perspective*. London: Routledge.

Zeki, S. (1993). *A Vision of the Brain*. Oxford: Blackwell.

INDEX